# WARD LOCKWOOD

# WARD LOCKWOOD

*1894 — 1963*

*Charles C. Eldredge*

THE UNIVERSITY OF KANSAS MUSEUM OF ART

LAWRENCE, KANSAS

*Cover:*

Detail of Ward Lockwood's *Kiowa Indian Dance*, 1940,
watercolor with waxed surface, 21 x 31½ inches, The
University of Kansas Museum of Art, The Lockwood Collection.

*Frontispiece:*

Ward Lockwood at the Hotel Don Fernando, Taos, New Mexico
Ward Lockwood Papers, Archives of American Art,
Smithsonian Institution, Washington, D. C.

*The publication of this study was made possible by a grant
from the Kansas University Endowment Association.*

Published in the United States of America in 1974
Copyright ☉ 1974 by The University of Kansas Museum of Art.
All rights reserved
Library of Congress Catalog Card Number: 74-17874
Miscellaneous Publications of The University of Kansas Museum of Art, No. 95
Printed by Vile-Goller/Fine Arts, Kansas City, Kansas

Designed by Ruth Lawner

*Photo Credits*

All works in the collection of The University of Kansas and the artist's estate were
photographed by James L. Enyeart and Terry Kafka. Other photographs are by
W. L. Bowers, Colorado Springs; Laura Gilpin; Peter A. Juley & Son, New York;
Patteson Studios, San Antonio; Phillips Studio, Philadelphia; Kenneth Schar, Santa Fe;
Stewart Bros., Washington, D. C.; Bill J. Strehorn, Dallas; and Ken Taylor, Kansas City,
Missouri

*For J. M. E.*

*The scientists' laboratories and the artists' studios, those havens of the quiet men, are much the same. Finding the new and fine in art constitutes fundamental research for the myriad of things we look at, use, enjoy daily. Discovering, inventing, finding new forms of beauty — feeding the dynamics of humanity — answering the demand for change, that constant of the universe — flashing light on the interminable path ahead — all these task the fine artist, [their] accomplishment . . . demands the dedication of an entire life.*

Ward Lockwood, 1955

# Contents

# Preface

Most prior discussions of Ward Lockwood's career have focused on his connections with Taos, New Mexico, and the colony of artists who worked there. This emphasis is understandable, for Lockwood himself freely admitted the strong attraction that place and those people had for him. Yet the painter's work is part of a larger context as well. The present study attempts to place his important Taos phase within an overall view of Lockwood's development.

That development covered more than four decades which were critical to the history of modern art. His early training and work in a quasi-impressionistic manner gave way to an approach that was more regional in nature. Later, in the years following World War II, Lockwood's art again became less regional in character, and he borrowed the abstract idiom of the period's avant-garde. His work, then, reflects the changing attitudes in American art over nearly half a century. The acclaim which he received during his lifetime attests to the successful blend of innovation and tradition which he effected.

It is particularly appropriate that this study originates on a university campus, for it was in such an environment that Lockwood spent much of his professional life. He was a professor at the Universities of Texas, California, Washington and Kansas, and in the campus ambience he found the combination of creative spirit and intellectual pursuit which nourished his art. Those of us fortunate enough to share such a situation can understand his choice.

This publication is fitting as well for the fact that the University of Kansas was Ward Lockwood's alma mater, and his ties to this school and this state remained strong throughout his life. Following his death the artist's estate was bequeathed to the Kansas University Endowment Association, which in turn donated a portion of the works to the University of Kansas Museum of Art. It is in conjunction with the unveiling of that bequest that this book is published.

This monograph about Ward Lockwood results from the generous cooperation of many persons. I am grateful to the individuals and museums who freely shared information regarding the artist's work in their collections. Of special interest and meaning were the recollections of Lockwood by his family, and by his friends, Emil Bisttram, Howard Cook, Andrew Dasburg, Gina Knee and Loren Mozley.

Written records often helped fill out the portrait of the artist sketched by his friends. Of greatest importance are the Lockwood Papers deposited at the Archives of American Art, and I am indebted to Garnett McCoy, Deputy Director-Archivist, and his staff for their assistance with these. I also appreciate the help of Harold T. Pinkett, Chief of the Natural Resources Branch of the Civil Archives Division, and James W. Moore, Director of the Audiovisual Archives Division, and their staffs at the National Archives; and of Martha Kehde, Art Librarian, and John Nugent, University Archivist, and their staffs at the University of Kansas Libraries.

Colleagues here and elsewhere have been supportive of my efforts. Adding to my understanding of Ward Lockwood were the insights of Patricia Trenton at the Denver Art Museum, of John Rothgeb at the University of Texas Drama Department, of Richard McKinzie at the University of Missouri — Kansas City, and Patric Shannon. For their patience and valuable advice I thank my assistant, David Curry; my typist, Margaret Etzenhouser, who cheerfully and ably prepared the manuscript; and my editor, Ruth Lawner, whose sharp eye and gentle hand were especially welcome.

The research for this publication was made possible by a grant from the Kansas University Endowment Association, whose support here as in other projects has been essential and most gratefully received.

*Lawrence, Kansas*
*July 12, 1974*

I-1: *Boats, ca.* 1902, watercolor, 7¾ x 9¾ inches, Estate of the artist

I-2: *Spirit of Christmas*, photograph courtesy Archives of American
Art, Smithsonian Institution

I-3: *United Fashion Show Poster, ca.* 1913, color lithograph, 21 x
13⅞ inches, The University of Kansas Museum of Art, The Lockwood Collection

# I. "An Artist's Roots"

Toward the end of his life, in looking back over a career of nearly half a century, Ward Lockwood described his main goal as a painter. On that occasion he wrote that "to paint poems, not to tell stories, is my objective."[1] The transition from the telling of stories to the painting of poems, from illustration to creative synthesis, can be understood as the main direction of Lockwood's career.

Born in Atchison, Kansas, on September 22, 1894, John Ward Lockwood was the elder son of Charles Alonzo and Cora Jane Lockwood. Charles Lockwood had come to Atchison from Michigan in 1885 to be associated with a local grocery firm. In 1890 he married Cora Jane Thomas, who had been reared by her grandparents in Atchison following the early death of her mother.

Although neither of his parents was an artist, they provided sympathetic support for their son's ambition toward a career as a painter. As recalled by Lockwood, "as far back as I can remember, a consuming desire to draw and paint pursued me. To become an artist has always been the goal, and I am grateful that my parents helped me in my efforts. One of my early thrills was a trip to the Chicago Art Institute with my father. Looming in that memory is the large painting, *The Bathers* by Bouguereau. Then how wonderful it seemed!"[2]

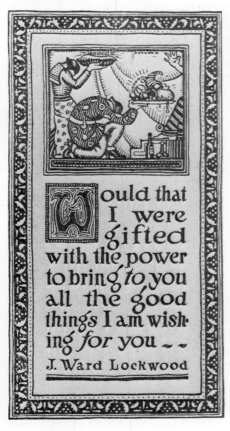

I-4: *Bookplate*,
Archives of American Art,
Smithsonian Institution

One of his father's bookkeepers, whose own artistic ambitions had somehow been frustrated, provided the young Ward with his first "instruction." As a youngster of seven or eight, Lockwood, with his teacher's help, produced small, Turner-like watercolors of Venetian boats with red sails, at least one of which he retained for the rest of his life (fig. I-1). Later, as a student in the Atchison schools, Lockwood continued to exercise his penchant for drawing and sketching with illustrations for various school and local publications. A drawing of the *Spirit of Christmas*, with Santa closing the door on Sickness, Murder and other demons, shows the heavy-handedness characteristic of many adolescent illustrators (fig. I-2).

Lockwood received his first extended instruction at the University of Kansas, with W. A. Griffith of the university's art department. Lockwood remembered Griffith as an excellent teacher who evidently encouraged his student's ambitions. It was during this period at the university that Lockwood began to gain some small success as a commercial artist, designing posters for Kansas City street cars (fig. I-3). In 1913 he won a third prize in the Kansas City Merchant's Association competition for a poster for their annual fashion show. Although the prize-winning design was scarcely innovative, it shows a command of basic principles and is thoroughly imbued with the spirit of its time. Designs for bookplates, greeting cards, and the like also occupied his time (fig. I-4), and by 1914 Lockwood had managed to save enough money from his commercial enterprises to permit him to go to Philadelphia to study at the Pennsylvania Academy of the Fine Arts.

11

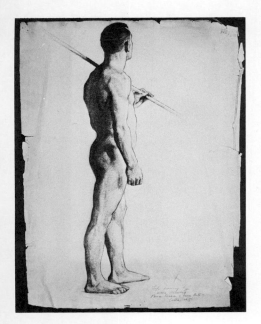

I-5: *Figure Study, ca.* 1915, charcoal, 24¼ x 18½ inches, Estate of the artist

In Philadelphia, young Lockwood entered the class taught by Henry McCarter. "The true principles of art and its wider meaning were taught by this man who was and is a potent force in American art," Lockwood recalled. McCarter "talked of Cézanne, van Gogh, the Armory Show, and introduced us to the whole exciting modern movement. I owe him a great deal."[3]

Among his fellow students at the Academy were Franklin Watkins and Abraham Rattner, and they and their classmates shared in the traditional discipline and curriculum which the school offered at that time. Henry McCarter may have introduced his students to "the whole exciting art movement," but little trace of this acquaintanceship appears in the surviving works from Lockwood's Philadelphia schooldays. A portfolio of life drawings does, however, show Lockwood's growing ability at handling the basic but difficult problems of the human form (fig. I-5). These explorations were continued in another vein with a series of animal sketches done at the Philadelphia Zoo about 1916 (fig. I-6). A sensitive sketch of the artist's mother done the following year shows Lockwood's continuing growth and the profitable results of his study at the Academy (fig. I-7). These studies, like those of many of his contemporaries, were to be interrupted in 1917 by America's entrance into World War I.

Although its overall effect on the course of American art may have been slight,[4] the European conflict did temporarily dislocate the lives and careers of many of our artists. The war had been a lively subject of debate among the students at the Pennsylvania Academy, as among Americans in general, and in 1917 Lockwood left Philadelphia to join the Army. Infected with patriotic spirit and by the ideal of a war to end all wars, he enlisted in April and served until his division was mustered out in 1919. During this period he fought in the battles of Argonne and St. Mihiel, and served with the Army of Occupation. Later he wrote: "That period now seems alternately a ghastly dream and an exciting adventure. The horror and abominable stupidity of war mingles in memory with the virility and dangerous excitement of its pageantry and action."[5]

I-6: *Lioness Studies, ca.* 1916, pencil, 7¼ x 11½ inches
  Estate of the artist

12

Charcoal drawing of my mother
Area 1917
Ward Lockwood

I-7: *Portrait of the Artist's Mother,*
*ca.* 1917, charcoal, 24¼ x 18½ inches,
Collection of Howard Lockwood

Lockwood did not make specific reference to it, but the post-armistice period in France must also have served to excite the imagination of the aspiring artist. While his station was along the Moselle, distant from the war-weary capital of Paris, Lockwood's military service did give him his first exposure to Europe, and his artistic imagination was doubtless quickened by the experience. As historians have noted, American involvement in the conflict drew this country into a world community, "and our art assumed, as did all art, a more international character," accelerating a tendency begun before the war.[6]

The interruption of world war made Lockwood's readjustment to peacetime and painting "confusing and frustrating at times. But," he wrote, "it was surprising and good to find that although paint and brushes had not been touched for many, many months, my work seemed to be actually a little more significant than before the long absence from the studio."[7]

13

With the experiences of Philadelphia training and European travel behind him, it was not surprising to find Lockwood returning to Paris in 1921 to pursue further his studies as an artist. Postwar Paris exercised a magnetic attraction for many American writers and painters of his generation, and Lockwood moved easily into the artists' community there. He shared a Montmartre studio with a fellow countryman and artist, Alexander Warshawsky, and enrolled at the Academie Ranson, where Maurice Denis and Jules Emile Zingg were teaching. He was disappointed to find the school's instruction "a repetition of what had already been experienced," and consequently pursued a program of independent study and painting.[8] The Louvre and the art galleries along the Rue de la Boetie became Lockwood's classroom. One of the high points of this Paris stay was the acceptance of a still-life painting in the Salon d'Automne (fig. I-8), although the artist confessed that "two hours were spent searching for it. Eventually it was discovered hung below the wainscoting."[9]

I-8: *Still Life*, 1921, oil on wood panel, 21½ x 15 inches,'
Estate of the artist

I-9: *Design with Figures, ca.* 1921, pencil, 13⅛ x 10⅛ inches, The University of Kansas Museum of Art, The Lockwood Collection

The richness and diversity of modern art available to the American student in Paris at that time was both stimulating and bewildering. To friends at home in Kansas, Lockwood admitted: "It is difficult to place a modern painter into any certain school of painting, because at the present time modern painting is so widely divergent. There are the 'Futurists,' the 'Cubists,' the 'Dada-ists,' and probably a score of other 'isms' and 'ists,' the names of which shall pass with the coming of a few years."[10]

Occasionally Lockwood's Parisian sketches suggest some efforts toward modernist designs (fig. I-9), but more frequently traces of advanced styles are lacking in the quick studies he made of the urban scene (figs. I-10, 11). In addition to its artistic activity, Lockwood also reacted to other aspects of French life. He recognized that "Paris is different now than it was during the war. There is not the life and gaiety here now that one felt after the armistice. As one walks through the Luxembourg or Tuilleries gardens, or through the Bois de Boulogne, he cannot escape from the feeling that Paris is like a beautiful woman convalescent from some serious illness. Because in the mourning worn by so many, many people and in their faces, one must read the traces of the sadness and terrible tragedy of the war. And I am quite sure that this aspect will only pass entirely with the coming of new generations."[11]

Given Lockwood's ambivalent attitude toward the Paris of the early 1920s, it can be readily understood that he left there after a short period for the sunnier climate of *Le Midi*. At Villeneuve-les-Avignon and at Cassis-sur-Mer, the winter of 1921-22 was passed with his fellow artist and fellow Kansan, Kenneth Adams.

I-10: *Garden Near Pont Neuf, ca.* 1921, pencil, 13⅛ x 10⅛ inches, The University of Kansas Museum of Art, The Lockwood Collection

I-11: *French Street Scene, ca.* 1921, pencil, 13⅛ x 10⅛ inches, The
University of Kansas Museum of Art, The Lockwood Collection

I-12: Paul Cézanne, *Le Golfe de Marseilles*, 1883-85, oil on canvas, 28¾ x 39½ inches, The Metropolitan Museum of Art, The H. O. Havemeyer Collection, Bequest of Mrs. H. O. Havemeyer, 1929

Lockwood described his work of that time as being "a mixture of Cézanne, van Gogh and Impressionism."[12] A typical painting from that winter, such as his *French Landscape, Avignon* (PLATE I), clearly shows the evidence of the first and the last. The strong sense of geometric form, seen in the rooftops and architectural blocks of the fore- and middle-grounds, derives from Cézanne. Lockwood utilized the elevated vantage point which encompasses a panoramic sweep of space, a device also employed in Cézanne's famed views of the Bay of Marseilles (fig. I-12). Yet humans are absent from Cézanne's structured view, and no invitation is made to enter the pictorial space; on the other hand, the roadway in Lockwood's scene, populated with carriages and figures, provides easy entry into the atmospheric distance, which is handled with an Impressionistic lack of definition. The young American here displays his divided loyalties, torn between the rational structure of Cézanne and the transient effects and gentler tones of the Impressionists.

The view of Avignon, like many of Lockwood's French canvases, was the result of direct observation and study of the subject. These paintings were often begun out of doors but were generally finished and retouched in the studio. It was there that the looseness and rapidity of his sketches was sacrificed for the strong formal qualities, so pro-

17

I-13: *Study for "Cassis sur Mer,"* 1922, pencil, Archives of American Art, Smithsonian Institution

nounced in the foreground of *French Landscape, Avignon.* A comparison of the sketches with the finished oils shows this propensity toward structure and geometry in the final work (figs. I-13, 14). During the winter in the South of France, Lockwood was frequently drawn to architectural subjects, including Roman arches and peasant cottages. He wrote fondly of "the quaint houses [which] bear the evidence of the age of the country. But yet there is a sense of ruggedness, of savageness, that lingers here and refuses to be obliterated."[13]

The time in France was well spent, and during this period Lockwood developed his handling of the oil medium considerably. His draughtsmanship improved; inspired especially by Cézanne and the rugged Provencal landscape, his feeling for structure and the organization of forms grew markedly. Despite his attraction to French subjects, however, Lockwood in 1922 returned to the United States "with the natural and not at all uncommon feeling of returning painters that one should work here where one's roots lie deep."[14]

The years immediately after his return were spent in Kansas City where, as in the immediate postwar period, he worked as a commercial artist. His drawings for advertisements offered a means of support, but scarcely provided the challenge and stimulation he had experienced while working with Adams in France (see fig. I-15). Lockwood chafed at the restraints of his occupation and later spoke of the role of the advertising illustrator with no trace of envy. "All that he does," stated Lockwood, "is geared to the materialistic side of our society. He must work against time to meet a publisher's deadline. He must

18

I-14: *Cassis sur Mer*, 1922, oil on canvas, 21¼ x 25½ inches, University
    Art Museum, University of California, Berkeley

I-15: *Advertisement for Skelly Oil*

subvert his skill to the business of selling a product. He must conform most of the time to the lowest common denominator of artistic appreciation because wide markets are a necessity to increased unit production. The excellence of his own product artistically has little to do with the success of his client's product. The idea of dollar profits so permeates the entire atmosphere of his surroundings that he cannot escape its pressure." As Lockwood developed his argument, his personal discomfort with the idea of advertising-illustration became more pronounced. It is difficult to avoid the conclusion that he was speaking autobiographically when he said that the illustrator "can only finally expire artistically to the commercial poison . . . In the commercial environment the artist-painter cannot long exist — that is to say he simply cannot live in the midst of such materialistic concepts or pressures. It is inimical to the whole process of fine art."[15]

Despite his distaste for the illustrator's profession, the Kansas City tenure was not without its highpoints. In 1922, upon his homecoming, he achieved a modicum of success with a one-man show of his French works at the Findlay Art Gallery in Kansas City. Occasional portrait commissions subsequently brought relief from the tedium of his advertising work. By 1926, his local reputation was such that Lockwood was selected to paint a "mural" of the old Kansas City Country Club.[16] This work — actually a large, framed oil painting on canvas (fig. I-16) — is scarcely distinctive as landscape painting, though the commission for it did certify Lockwood's standing in the Kansas City community. The experience of working on mural-sized painting was to become more familiar to Lockwood and many other American artists in the next decade in the Roosevelt administration's New Deal art projects.

The most significant event in Lockwood's life following his return to the Middle West was his 1924 marriage to Miss Clyde Bonebrake, the daughter of a prominent Topeka family. It was her support and encouragement that finally led Lockwood to the decision that, "come what may, my painting was to be our first concern. I resigned from the [advertising] agency and we turned the nose of an old Velie automobile toward the fabulous village of Taos, New Mexico."[17] It was there in the community of Taos painters that Ward Lockwood was to embark upon the second and most familiar phase of his career.

I-16: *View of the Old Kansas City Country Club*, 1926, oil on canvas, Kansas City Country Club

20

# II.  Taos: Creative Freedom

"We came here when Taos was a three-bathroom town."[1] Thus did Mrs. Lockwood recall the New Mexico settlement which she and her husband encountered in 1926. Rustic though the town and its plumbing may have appeared to the new arrivals, it was that same unspoiled quality which lent Taos much of its charm.

From the middle years of the nineteenth century, artists had been drawn to the rugged landscape of northern New Mexico. The earliest visitors to paint the area were generally in the company of military expeditions. Subsequently some of our best-known landscapists toured and depicted the region, such as Worthington Whittredge in 1865 and Thomas Moran in the 1880s. These pioneers were attracted by the novel and surprising beauty of the landscape, so different from the familiar terrain of the Atlantic coast or the Middle West. Oscar Blumenschein, one of the charter members of the Taos art colony, recorded his first impressions of the fabled Taos Valley: "The color, the effective character of the landscape, the drama of the vast spaces, the superb beauty and severity of the hills stirred one deeply . . . "[2] Like others in the first generation of Taos painters, Blumenschein delighted in the variety of pictorial material readily available in the vicinity of Taos. He later recalled: "When I came into this valley — for the first time in my life, I saw whole paintings right before my eyes. Everywhere I looked I saw paintings perfectly organized, ready to paint."[3]

The area was not without its detractors, however. Stuart Davis came to New Mexico, struggled with the area, and left, momentarily defeated by the scale of the place. Others did not even try to cope with the unique possibilities of the New Mexican scene; Jules Pascin is reported to have stepped off the train there and immediately reboarded, exclaiming that the sunlight was too intense for him. Maurice Sterne was perhaps the most outspoken in his distaste for Taos: "I did not like Taos from the moment I set foot there. I felt its void, a primeval space before concrete form began to take shape. It not only failed to stimulate my own powerful sense of form, the absence was like an ache that made me feel empty myself. There was a loneliness about the place which I physically suffered."[4]

As Frieda Lawrence noted, "You love the place or you don't; there's no middle way . . . either you belong or you don't."[5] Despite the reactions to the contrary, most artists, both seasonal visitors and permanent residents, could not escape the powerful charm which the Taos country exerted. For some, the attraction was evidence of what Malcolm Cowley defined as a "nostalgia for the primitive that had played such a large part not only in contemporary letters but in contemporary life as well."[6] The primeval terrain of northern New Mexico provided a "last frontier," an escape from the growing complexities of life in urban America. On occasion this nostalgia for the primitive led to the development of a strong concept of "spirit of place" and a stress upon the mystique of Taos. Especially for the first-generation painters, the colorful presence of the Pueblo Indians added to the unique appeal of Taos and offered frequent subjects for their canvases.

Several of these painters of Indians came to their work from backgrounds as illustrators, and in their Pueblo portraits and depictions of Indian life they betray a romanticism which occasionally lapses into sentimentality. One of them, Bert Phillips, explained his artistic inspiration: "As I visit their villages and talk with my Indian friends I see and hear the young bucks wrapped in their white blankets standing on the bridge singing a love song in the moonlight and I feel the romance of youth . . . I believe that it is the romance of this great pure-aired [sic] land that makes the most lasting impression on my mind and heart."[7]

In 1912, Phillips was among the six founding members of the Taos Society of Artists, at least half of whom are best remembered for their work in the Indian genre. The Society brought the first formal recognition to the artist's colony which had been developing in Taos since the turn of the century. As explained by one of its members, "Art at this time had not crossed the Mississippi westward. Men creating it lived in eastern states because they felt the need of close association with both dealers and museums . . . Consequently, a group of painters living in a little New Mexico village isolated from the main current of art activity, working with material until then little exploited, and setting themselves up as an exhibiting society stirred the imagination of critical reviewers and writers of art."[8]

The Taos Society of Artists continued its lively role in the life of the colony until 1927. Among the artists who were lured to the town during those years, and the last member to join the Society before its disbandment, was Kenneth Adams. It was Adams with whom Ward Lockwood had painted in the south of France in the early 1920s, and in the subsequent correspondence between the two men, Adams had written glowingly of his new life in Taos. Later, Lockwood recalled that "Kenneth Adams had written us letters extolling Taos as a place to live and work, and in as much as we were much more familiar with the eastern seaboard and countries abroad than with our own west, we decided to spend three or four months in New Mexico."[9] Thus it was that the Lockwood's arrived in "three-bathroom Taos" on an April evening in 1926.

The first months in New Mexico were stimulating ones for the Lockwoods, filled with introductions to the marvelous countryside and its equally fascinating inhabitants. "During that exciting summer we became acquainted with so many people, all friendly, all different — real individualists. We discovered country new and wild and strange to us."[10]

However stimulating the company of "real individualists" and the pace of Taos social life, it was the novel and compelling landscape which held the greatest excitement and meaning for the artist. Lockwood once explained that Taos offered the perfect home for the artist; but unlike some earlier painters, this was "not because it is the home of the

II-1: *French Landscape*, 1922, oil on canvas, 25¾ x 32 inches, Museum of Fine Arts, Boston

Indians. That is incidental. It is the landscape that sets Taos apart from and above other haunts of the artist."[11]

Lockwood's strong personal reaction to the Taos landscape was suggested in the freshness and vigor with which he painted the countryside during his first summer there. By the end of that stay, Lockwood had capitulated to the peculiar charms of Taos and its surroundings; the seasonal visitor decided to make Taos his home. At summer's end in 1926, the Lockwoods purchased an old adobe structure which had at one time served as a Penitente *morada*, and they remodeled this house the following summer. In 1928, Lockwood added a studio to the home, where he and his wife continued to reside until 1939.

When the paintings of his first New Mexico summer were exhibited the following winter, they elicited the praise of both critics and public. "Mr. Lockwood enlivens the hackneyed subjects of the Taos colony," wrote one Kansas City reviewer, "until one is almost willing to be convinced that it is a paintable country after all. A whole exhibition by a Taos artist and only one Indian! Bravo!"[12]

Although differing in important respects, such as topography, and the quality of light, there are nevertheless some parallels between the landscapes which Lockwood produced in the South of France in 1922 and those which he brought back from Taos four years later. The *French Landscape* of 1922 (fig. II-1) and his *Haying Time in Talpa* of

1926 (PLATE II) both present light-filled, rural landscapes, with road-ways and building forms indicating recession into the distance. In the earlier work, however, the buildings are both more numerous and more severely geometrical, reflecting the Cézannesque spirit in which they were painted. The New Mexico haying scene, by contrast, is more boldly and loosely painted.

The Talpa picture was the star of Lockwood's 1927 exhibition. One critic praised Lockwood's success "in giving a refreshing original conception of the Taos community — a feat which is the more remarkable in view of the well-worn popularity of the subject. Instead of squaws and burros and striped shawls he presents this great expanse of summer landscape [in *Haying Time in Talpa*] . . . It is an intimate, personal document, full of the flavor of the countryside."[13] Maynard Walker wrote that the painting presented "a portrait of a landscape, put down with a fine discrimination in the use of bold color, and an understanding regard for the essentials that underline all form. It is witty, exuberant, and sincere."[14]

Lockwood's "regard for the essentials that underline all form" is a reflection of his earlier landscape studies in a Cézannesque vein, in which the organization and structure of the landscape elements were of paramount importance. This rigorous training, pursued during his Provencal sojourn of 1921-22, continued to influence his later New Mexican landscapes. At the same time, however, new considerations occupied the artist's attention; the wondrous landscape of Taos inspired a more direct, spontaneous and less self-consciously studied response than did the Mediterranean terrain he had previously painted. The artist admitted that Taos and its surroundings must be "felt rather than described."[15]

Through Kenneth Adams, Lockwood was introduced to Andrew Dasburg who was to be a major influence on his work of the Taos period. Dasburg, born in Paris in 1887, had reversed the usual pattern by coming to America where he studied in Robert Henri's night classes in New York, and with Birge Harrison in Woodstock, New York. In 1907 he had returned to Paris where he visited with Matisse, Leo Stein, Vollard, and other leaders of the contemporary avant-garde; it was also in the course of this French sojourn that Dasburg became infected with an enthusiasm for the work of Cézanne. Dasburg later recalled: " . . . a great elevation of spirit . . . I experienced, by chance, one day when I walked down a little Paris street. I came upon a small gallery where, in the window, were three or four paintings by Cézanne whose work I had heard mentioned but knew nothing of. I was immediately impressed by the great plastic reality of the paintings . . . The gallery was hung with Cézannes. I looked for a long time . . . I was completely imbued with what I saw — one of those experiences which rarely happen but when they do, are forever memorable."[16] After Paris and the discovery of Cézanne, Dasburg returned to this country and settled in Woodstock, where he helped establish the Woodstock Art Association and Gallery. It was from that New York art colony that Dasburg, in 1916, left for his summer's visit to Taos. He followed Maurice Sterne and his wife, Mabel Dodge Sterne, to that New Mexico settlement, where he returned annually before permanently settling there in 1930.

Kenneth Adams had studied under Dasburg in Woodstock in 1919 and 1920, and it was the teacher who directed his student to the wonders of Taos, which he had only discovered a few years earlier. Adams migrated to New Mexico in 1924, where he continued to work alongside his mentor.

Dasburg's influence was not limited to Adams and Lockwood. Indeed, many observers have spoken of the forceful impression which Dasburg made upon nearly all of his students, and on other painters as well. "From the early years of his career he had a curious power over other artists. It almost seemed he had a magic hand that drew from the student the potential creativeness that so often is unawakened and lies dormant a whole life through. He was able to communicate his own gift of seeing and stimulate in others the faculty so strongly developed in himself. He was really, from the first, a born teacher . . ."[17] In a tribute to the artist, Lockwood wrote: " . . . I know of no single artist in the Southwest who has influenced, or does influence, the work of younger painters more than Andrew Dasburg."[18]

Lockwood's early Taos views show this relation to Dasburg's work. With their shared affinity for Cézanne, it is not surprising to discover a sense for regular organization of forms within the composition. With both artists, however, the severity of Cézanne's style is modified by the different nature of the New Mexican countryside. Lockwood's debt to Dasburg can be seen in his expansive landscapes across the Taos Valley. In *Women in the Fields, Taos*, (fig. II-2)[19] Lockwood is concerned with the same broad sweep of space, viewed from an elevated vantage point, as he had depicted in *Haying Time in Talpa*. The former painting, however, uses a tighter, more structured composition in the middle ground which suggests the link to Dasburg, and through him to Cézanne. This tendency toward a highly structured, checkerboard patterning of the Taos fields is seen in many of Dasburg's landscapes from the mid-twenties (fig. II-3), and became increasingly evident in Lockwood's work of subsequent years.

The colorful building and mountain forms of Lockwood's *Turn in the Road, Old Ledoux Street*, 1928 (PLATE III), are more organic than geometric in nature. In this they reflect the irregular qualities of the adobe architecture and the rugged landscape common to the region. The tilting forms, with verticals slightly askew, convey the convulsive feeling of an incomplete landscape, a landscape in the process of becoming. This quality of the terrain inspired strong responses from artists. "Taos Valley seemed to me like the first days of creation . . . ," exclaimed Dasburg on his first acquaintance with the landscape.[20]

The irregularity of Taos' adobe architecture also lent charm to the village. Mabel Dodge (Sterne) Luhan proudly claimed that "The 'line' here is not mechanical. We do nothing rigidly here. The eye decides, and the walls of our houses are not so very plumb."[21] Later she was to ask, "who knows what influence was exerted upon the [visiting artist] by these adobe buildings, built without benefit of plumb line or water level: thick, uneven walls, windows askew, doors out of kilter? There was a curious handmade quality to everything about one here in those long-ago days, and everything was a little casual, intimate, and at times fantastic."[22]

25

II-2: *Women in the Fields, Taos, ca.*
1926, oil on canvas, 20 x 24 inches,
Estate of the artist

II-3: Andrew Dasburg, *Taos Valley, ca.* 1926, oil on artist's board,
13 x 16¼ inches, The University of Kansas Museum of Art,
The Lockwood Collection

II-4: *Taos Signs, ca.* 1929, oil on canvas, 30¼ x 35¼ inches, University
Art Museum, University of New Mexico, Albuquerque

II-5: Andrew Dasburg, *Taos Plaza*, oil on canvas, 13 x 16¼ inches,
location unknown, photograph courtesy Dallas Museum of Fine Arts

The business and social life of this unique community centered around the Taos plaza. Overrun today with tourists and businesses catering to them, the Taos plaza in the 1920s was quite a different sight. The town was without electric power, without water systems, without sewers, and without telephones, except for a single private line linking it to the outside world. Lockwood recalled that "At night, candles and coal lamps lit most of the houses. Stars lit the streets . . . A few drooping strands of barbed wire hanging from leaning cedar posts and wobbly hitching rails marked the unpaved road around the plaza.[23] . . . [T]he adobe mud in the little plaza would suck the galoshes off a tenderfoot's feet."[24]

The plaza which Lockwood described became a recurrent theme in his work about 1929. Like other artists of the community, Lockwood was attracted to this subject by its colorful blend of Spanish, Indian, and American cultures, by the excitement of the crowds and by the variety and gaiety of the signs and storefronts there. But whereas some other Taos artists sought to record the scene in a straightforward, documentary way, Lockwood's *Taos Signs* of *ca.* 1929 (fig. II-4) is more active in its composition and more expressive of the liveliness of the plaza. At least one critic commented upon this aspect of Lockwood's painting. Regarding *Taos Signs*, he wrote: "Though contemporary painting is full of lettering, used for all sorts of purposes, what other artist has thought of painting the portraits of signs? Each is like a personal signature, differing from the others as only signatures can. Swaggering along the street, they not only advertise their wares but say something too of the natures of the men who put them there."[25]

In this painting, Lockwood's interest in the jazzy rhythms of the signs parallels that of his friend Dasburg, whose *Taos Plaza* (fig. II-5) is identical in subject. The choppy visual accents and the manner in which Lockwood centralizes the image of his *Taos Signs*, angling and leaving blank the corners of the canvas, evoke comparisons as well with the work of John Marin. Although Lockwood seems to have been independently disposed toward such visually activated imagery, his introduction to Marin in 1929 certainly accentuated that direction in his work.

Marin came to Taos as the guest of Mabel Dodge Luhan, the community's colorful and often controversial hostess and publicist (fig. II-6). Marin had heard much of the fabled New Mexican landscape from his many painter-friends who had preceded him there, and it is probable that he traveled to the Southwest in hopes of tackling some of the basic pictorial problems of modern landscape painting. A year before his introduction to Taos, Marin had written: "Seems to me the true artist must perforce go from time to time to the elemental big forms — Sky, Sea, Mountains, Plains — . . . to sort of re-true himself up, to recharge the battery."[26] The Taos landscape, which had been so vividly described to him by Marsden Hartley, Mrs. Luhan and others, would provide him with "elemental big forms" aplenty during the two summers of 1929 and 1930 which he spent there.

Marin's New Mexico journey owes a debt as well to the same aversion to urban life which drove many other artists and intellectuals out of New York and to remote colonies, like Taos, during those years. As

II-6: *Caricature of Mabel Dodge Luhan,* pen and ink, The Archives of American Art, Smithsonian Institution

II-7: *August Bargain Days*, watercolor, 13-7/8 x 19-15/16 inches,
Marion Koogler McNay Art Institute, Bequest of Marion Koogler
McNay

described by one biographer, Marin in 1929 "was tired of 'living in
herds,' of swimming in a 'common pool.' He found it hard to keep
the spirit unsoiled in the pool."[27] For such weariness Taos offered an
antidote; as Lockwood noted, " . . . the place was remote from the
frenzied fantasies of the urban twenties."[28]

Although the Taos community was, by the late 1920s, well
accustomed to visiting celebrities, it was still with some excitement
that John Marin was received as a summer guest. As recalled by his
hostess, Marin "came and saw and conquered. He conquered not
only the landscape, but many of the resident artists. The summer after
he was here, one saw traces of Marin's method and technique in many
canvases of the younger men, who tried to learn from him and to see
with his eyes, and, in part, succeeded."[29]

Marin's closest Taos friendships developed not within Mabel
Luhan's circle, which one Taoseno described as very "mystical" and
not really at the center of the artist's community.[30] Instead, Marin
shared easily in the camaraderie and life style of Andrew Dasburg,
Ward Lockwood and their associates. Loren Mozley, a younger member

of this group, recalled its special spirit with fondness. "This was a good time," he wrote. "We were in our twenties, at an altitude of seven thousand feet — you can imagine! There were days of fly-fishing in the pools and riffles of the Hondo, unforgettable days, and a night of choking campfire and whiskey and pork and beans down at the box canyon. We sketched black-and-white ducks together through the red willows around Pilar. And Andrew saved one foolhardy youngster from the Rio Grande in icy midwinter. Books were shared and there were games of chess or bridge, and conversation and argument before a pinon fire in the Lockwood living room. Our corduroys were washed in the same suds. We knew all the same picturesque neighbors. And about us was the superb landscape, green and sage-gray, or covered with snow and blue — the same inviting, open countryside. Our world was small and we knew each other."[31]

Ward Lockwood shared similar memories of their small world, and of John Marin who briefly entered it." . . . Andrew Dasburg, Loren Mozley, and I knew every trout pool in the Rio Hondo; knew every rock, bump and gully that slowed our progress thereto; knew the bootleggers who manufactured and provided us with 'Taos Lightning,' that elixir of corn which warmed us after wading hip deep in the melted snows of trout streams. We were part of a kind of painter-fisherman clan that seems to exist universally. It didn't take long for us to know that Marin was a member, too."[32]

The group that fished together, painted together; and Marin's excitement and intrigue with the Taos landscape equalled that of his friends. In New Mexico Marin confined himself to watercolor, the difficult medium whose possibilities Lockwood had begun to explore about 1928. The unique dynamic which Marin captured in his water-colors left its mark on his Taos protégés, and Lockwood's watercolor views of the plaza have an even crisper and more active quality than the oil painting, *Taos Signs*. In *August Bargain Days* (fig. II-7) and *Street Scene, Taos* (PLATE IV) can be seen the shifting, dancing strokes of color and the lively contest of forms which were characteristic of Lockwood's views of the town at that time.

The change in style in the watercolors cannot be attributed solely to Marin's influence; the different nature of the medium played a role as well. In a comparison of Lockwood's *New Mexico Town*, painted in oil about 1926-28 (fig. II-8), with his 1932 watercolor, *Exciting Winter Day* (fig. II-9) can be seen the transition undergone by the artist in that period. The heavier, emphatically geometric forms of the oil give way to more stacatto rhythms and less insistently solid forms in the later watercolor.

Although he was at the time speaking of his friend Victor Higgins' conversion to the watercolor medium, Lockwood's comments seem to have an autobiographical meaning as well. Lockwood wrote that Higgins "turned from his habitual brushstrokes of oil and ventured into an extended series of watercolors . . . In my opinion this was a happy and important change in his painting as well as a richly rewarding experience which enhanced the quality of his later work. The more direct medium was for him a new challenge and a release . . . The medium opened a door through which he escaped a certain boredom

II-8: *New Mexico Town, ca.* 1926-28, oil on canvas, 24 x 32 inches,
The University of Kansas Museum of Art, The Lockwood Collection

II-9: *Exciting Winter Day*, 1932, watercolor, 13½ x 19 inches, Estate
of the artist

II-10: *Arroyo Seco*, 1933, oil on canvas, 30 x 40 inches, The University of Kansas Museum of Art, The Lockwood Collection

with the weightiness of oil impasto. He found the lighter medium sympathetic to the more lyrical side of his nature."[33] As did Higgins, so too did Lockwood discover a new freedom and an expressive possibility in watercolor which he had not previously realized in his oils.

On occasion Lockwood did try to translate the sketchy forms and abbreviated brushstrokes of the watercolors into the less tractable oil medium, as in his *Arroyo Seco* of 1933 (fig. II-10). In other oils Lockwood made extensive use of the palette knife to spread the pigment with greater force. His *Rio Hondo* of 1930 (PLATE V), as with the watercolor views of the Taos Valley, is marked by a grand sense of space and scale which typify the region and help explain its attraction. Lockwood would have agreed with Marin that "The country is so damn big — so that if you succeed in expressing a little — one ought to be satisfied and proceed to pat oneself."[34]

It was in the watercolors, however, that Lockwood most successfully captured the spirit and drama of the New Mexican landscape. His colleague, Andrew Dasburg, wrote that it was Lockwood's "watercolors [which] keep coming to mind. They for me are the very apex of his art . . ."[35]

At one time Lockwood claimed that his love for Taos was based on the wealth and variety of pictorial materials, including the people, the large landscape, and the expansive and colorful skies which crown the valley. In giving an idea of the scale of the area, Lockwood noted: "At times I have seen as many as seven storms forming in the skies at the same time."[36] This spaciousness and the sense of nature's power are conveyed in Lockwood's *Dark Mountain and Storm* (fig. II-11),

32

in which the watercolor washes are heavily applied, suggestive of the dampness of the storm itself. The sense of great space in the landscape, emphasized by the vacant fore- and middle-grounds, is like that of Marin's *Storm Over Taos* of 1930 (fig. II-12), to which the Lockwood bears a certain parallel. However, the younger man's picture is overall more freely handled, without the schematic quality of Marin's clouds and lightning.

The spaciousness of the landscape, at times awesome, was nearly inescapable. After fifty years there, the painter Dorothy Brett can still say with genuine amazement, as she surveys the valley from her home: "The country is *so big* — it's impossible!"[37] Lockwood also made continual reference to this quality of the landscape. In his journal he wrote of the Little Rio Grande Canyon, calling it "a terrifying — gorgeous piece of nature! Little surprising things — sage bushes, rocks, piercing trees, delicate color — all happening within the big sharp cut forms of the canyon walls — in a tremendous stretch of space."[38] This journal entry's combination of close study of forms — rocks, trees, bushes — and cognizance of vast spaces is reflected in some of the paintings of this period as well. Lockwood's *Hondo Canyon* (fig. II-13) is divided vertically into two areas; on the left side is the view to the distant peak, while on the right side, the painter examines the abstract patterns established in the foreground cliffs. This split focus, with its dual emphasis on near and far, and the search for abstract designs within the natural scene, suggest further parallels with Marin's Taos watercolors.

That Lockwood should have found inspiration in the work of Marin is scarcely surprising, as the latter was then beginning to achieve acclaim as one of the leading American modernists. The relationships between their work did not escape the critics of the period. In May, 1931, Lockwood's Taos paintings were exhibited at the Rehn Galleries in New York; one critic, commenting upon his "Marinesque water-colors," found them to be "much more tangible, much less surrealistic than Marin. He is less mystifying, he gives more of the actual scene before him with, however, a special emotional response in each annotation."[39] The *New York Sun* found that Lockwood's "individ-ualism, hitherto so invincible, shows slight tendencies to Marinitis." Given Marin's major position, however, the critic did not find this unusual, and he admitted that the tendency was not pronounced and had to do with choice of motif, not with technique.[40] One reviewer went so far as to praise Lockwood in contrast to the master: "He has taken some notes from Marin, to be sure. But though it may be heresy to say so, he strikes us as close to the latter in skill, and somewhat more pictorially interesting. His style is spotty rather than smooth or fluent, but the effect is sparklingly vivid and harmonious."[41]

Whether the commentary was favorable or otherwise, the artist was most pleased when the critics approached his work on its own merits, without reference to other artists. Sending some reviews home from New York, he wrote: "Here are some of the knocks and boosts that were in the papers this weekend. Altogether I think the show was well noticed — all of them [the critics] said it was unique — I was glad they did not liken me to any other painter."[42]

33

II-11: *Dark Mountain and Storm*, watercolor, 18½ x 24½ inches,
Estate of the artist

II-12: John Marin, *Storm Over Taos, New Mexico*, 1930, watercolor,
15 x 20-15/16 inches, National Gallery of Art, Washington, D. C.,
Alfred Stieglitz Collection

II-13: *Hondo Canyon*, watercolor, 13½ x 19 inches, Estate of the artist

Despite the limitations of New Mexican regionalism, and the fervent, "mystical" defenses and descriptions of Taos offered by Mabel Dodge Luhan, there remained there in the 1930s a core of modern easel painters who continued their essays involving the formal problems of landscape painting. As during the preceding decade, Andrew Dasburg remained the center of this group. In spite of the economic difficulties of the time, painters continued to migrate seasonally to the region, perhaps attracted as much by its relatively economical living as by the storied landscape; whatever their inspiration for travel there, the summer sojourns (or longer) of Emil Bisstram, Yasuo Kuniyoshi, Gina Knee, Cady Wells, Rebecca Strand, and others continued to add variety and new ideas to the Taos community.

It was during this critical decade, in such an environment, that Ward Lockwood entered his maturity as an artist. His experiences of the 1920s remained important, and evidences of Cézanne- or Dasburg-like structural concerns and of Marinesque brushwork reappear in certain paintings of the 1930s; however, these devices gradually become better integrated into Lockwood's personal style, until his best work is ultimately able to transcend its influence.

At the same time, other earlier borrowings are dropped from his vocabulary. In the early 1930s, for instance, the subtle Impressionist tonalities of Lockwood's first landscapes were abandoned in favor of emphatic contrasts of light and dark. Many of the paintings which utilized this new value scale were winter landscapes. These paintings

III-1: *Midwinter, ca.* 1933, oil on canvas, Addison Gallery of American Art, Andover, Massachusetts

III-2: *Taos Plaza in Snow, ca.* 1933, oil on canvas, 30 x 40 inches, The Pennsylvania Academy of the Fine Arts, Lambert Fund Purchase

echo the spirit and color of Mabel Dodge Luhan's description of winter in Taos: " . . . now, in the frozen immunity of winter, the earth on either side of the road looks like blue glaciers interminably stretching to the mountain slopes, monotonously still except for a sudden splash of black, when a couple of crows land on the dark huddle of a carcass, for horses and cows fall and die throughout the cold months and are devoured in a few hours."[6]

Her stark description is matched by the stark contrasts of Lockwood's *Magic of the Snows* of 1934 (PLATE VI), or *Midwinter* (fig. III-1). The forms in each are extremely simplified, with the latter's being more dense than those of the former; this is, perhaps, due to the greater density of the oil pigment used in the latter painting. But even with the sketchy, Marin-like calligraphy of the watercolor, the startling play of dark against light gives the picture a boldness and structural strength which it shares with *Midwinter*. The artist recorded his thoughts regarding this factor. "Have done several more or less important canvases since returning to Taos in November," he wrote in his journal," — *Taos Street, The Plaza in Snow* [fig. II-2], watercolor of the *Turtle Dance*, and the winter landscape with a large black crow. All of some import probably because they are examples of the development of a black and white range in the palette — something I have been conscious of for at least two years. — A very important thing I believe is this black and white palette range — that is a dark and light breadth of scale. Most of the Impressionists were responsible for a neglect of this — playing most of the time in a tonal fog — ignoring the value of a sharp contrast to enhance a tonal passage. Ignoring also the passages of white between color areas — passages which allow certain combinations of color to play against themselves — like the passages between rests in music."[7]

The growing mastery and independent control that Lockwood developed in his pictures of the early 1930s, coupled with his exhibition awards in Chicago, San Francisco, Denver, and elsewhere, helped advance his name and work before the public's attention. The growth in personal reputation, however, coincided with the decline in the nation's economic fortunes. "The great depression was slow in making its effect evident in the rural community of Taos," recalled Lockwood, "but as months passed by painters felt the blow as the art market practically disappeared."[8] Thus it was for financial as well as artistic reasons that in 1932 Lockwood eagerly accepted a summer teaching job at the Broadmoor Art Academy in Colorado Springs. The Colorado school was under the direction of Boardman Robinson, who during the 1930s attracted to its faculty a number of talented men and women to serve as visiting instructors and guest artists. Among them were Lockwood and his friends Adams and Dasburg, as well as Thomas Hart Benton, George Biddle, Arnold Blanch, Paul Burlin, Adolf Dehn, Ernest Fiene, Doris Lee, Peppino Mangravite, Frank Mechau, and Henry Varnum Poor.

At Broadmoor, during the summers of 1932, 1933, and 1934, Lockwood taught landscape painting and also lithography (fig. III-3). His courses in lithography were an innovation for the Colorado school. Lockwood's own work in this medium began in the late 1920s, roughly coinciding with the revival of interest in lithography nationwide.

III-3: *Pike's Peak From Colorado Springs*, lithograph, 12 x 17 inches, The University of Kansas Museum of Art, The Lockwood Collection

III-4: *Taos Hotel Facade*, 1929, lithograph,
10 x 13½ inches, The University of Kansas
Museum of Art, The Lockwood Collection

III-5: *Taos Signs*, 1929, lithograph, 12½ x 16 inches,
The University of Kansas Museum of Art,
The Lockwood Collection

The early lithographs of Taos were printed in small, often unnumbered
editions. A view such as the *Taos Hotel Facade*, 1929 (fig. III-4) is
basically an exercise in verticals and horizontals; the stable balance of
the architectural form, centered within the composition, is quite unlike
the jazzy rhythms which typified Lockwood's paintings of the plaza,
done at the same time. The plaza paintings, however, like *Taos Signs*
(fig. II-4), also served as the models for the lithographs of the same
type (fig. III-5). Except for minor changes in some of the figures and
automobiles, the *Taos Signs* print is a virtual copy of the oil, done in
the same year.

III-6: *Summer Landscape, Taos, N. M.*, watercolor, 13-15/16 x 20 inches, Marion Koogler McNay Art Institute, Bequest of Marion Koogler McNay

For the most part, Lockwood's lithographs present the same solutions to problems of landscape as seen in the paintings with which they were contemporaneous. Unlike his later work with collography, there was little innovation attempted with the unique qualities of the graphic medium. When they have been shown — which is less frequently than the oils and watercolors — they have been praised as being "done with expertness and finesse"; however, at the same time it was recognized that the lithographs "are, of course, quieter in mood than his watercolors."[9] Although technically adept, the lack of conceptual boldness in the lithographs probably reflects Lockwood's lesser experience in the medium.

The seasons in Colorado Springs gave Lockwood his first exposure to classroom teaching. It was in this role that he was subsequently to perform for more than twenty years. Although before Broadmoor he had not formally taught, he had in 1931 advised and assisted Gina Knee; she had been drawn to Taos that year by her enthusiasm for the western landscapes of John Marin exhibited in New York in 1930. Knee recalls Lockwood's "open cordial personality" with fondness, but

III-7: Gina Knee, *Near Cordova, N. M.*, 1943, watercolor, 19 x 23 inches, Larcada Gallery, New York

feels that his greatest importance to her was as a model of an artist's lifestyle, rather than as an aesthetic influence.[10] Whether due to his personality or his artistic theory, there does appear to be a relationship established between the works of advisor and advisee, "teacher" and "student," as seen in a comparison of Lockwood's *Summer Landscape, Taos* (fig. III-6) and Knee's *Near Cordova, New Mexico* (fig. III-7). In its rapid, sketchy technique and abbreviated style, the latter's work seems to derive from the former, and also to reflect her admiration for Paul Klee's fanciful constructions.

While his personal and artistic example affected Knee and others in New Mexico and Colorado, Lockwood continued to develop his own interpretations of his Taos home. In the mid-1930s, in the depths of the great depression, the market for modern pictures slowed — although by no means did popular interest in the arts slacken. Indeed, the art programs of the Roosevelt administration served to broaden significantly the base of support and interest in the arts. The mural commissions offered by the federal government came to occupy a major portion of Lockwood's concern during these years. (See chapter IV.)

III-8: *Taos Today*, 1934, oil on canvas, 36 x 48 inches, The University
of Kansas Museum of Art, The Lockwood Collection

Despite his involvement with mural programs, Lockwood did not abandon entirely his easel painting. One of his best-known pictures is *Taos Today*, which he painted in 1934 (fig. III-8). This large oil painting is the summation of Lockwood's series of Taos plaza studies, dating back to *circa* 1928. The 1934 canvas developed logically from precedents such as the *Taos Plaza in Snow* (fig. III-2) of the preceding year; both paintings combine areas of rather free brushwork, especially in the foliage, with heavily impastoed areas of ground and sky. In the earlier picture the artist has made use of the palette knife to build up his paint surface, a technique Dasburg had used on occasion, and which Lockwood was to repeat in his works of the 1940s and 1950s.

Compositionally, both paintings have a common subject — the Taos plaza — framed on the left by the same architectural elements. Yet the earlier picture's extensive view beyond the plaza to the mountains is blocked in the later work by foliage, architecture and signs. The space in *Taos Today* is less continuous, appearing more like a series of stage flats dropped across the plaza. In this regard it suggests parallels to Stuart Davis' town- and cityscapes of a few years earlier, although Lockwood unfortunately left no comments regarding his opinion of Davis. *Taos Today* also shows strong parallels to the work of Boardman Robinson, especially in the caricatured figures at the left. Lockwood wrote that he and Robinson "became steadfast friends" during his summers in Colorado Springs, and the example of Robinson's illustrational style seems to have made its impact on *Taos Today*. Although it differs markedly in subject, the latter's *Entombment* (fig. III-9) shows a similar handling of human anatomy and an inten-

III-9: Boardman Robinson, *The Entombment*, 1935, wash and pencil touched with white, 9½ x 13½ inches, The Dallas Museum of Fine Arts, Gift of Summerfield Roberts

tional crudity in drawing technique; in this case, the compositions of the two pictures are even similar, with standing figures at the left acting as parentheses to the prominent, hunched figure in the foreground. This particular Robinson drawing, dating from 1935, may of course have been influenced by the Lockwood. More fruitful, however, than arguments over who preceded whom, is the recognition of a shared sensibility common to these two artists working in close collaboration during Lockwood's several summers at Broadmoor.

The dual delights of fishing and landscape painting continued to occupy the Taos painters into the mid- and late-1930s, as time from mural commissions and other responsibilities permitted. It was during this decade that this country's fascination with and allegiance to its native subject matter led to the high tide of American Scene painting. Senator Robert M. LaFollette, Jr., reflected a national attitude which prized native subjects. In opening an exhibition of work done under the Treasury Department's Section of Fine Arts, LaFollette commented: "I find a particular interest in the galleries because they present the work of artists living in every region of this great country . . . I like to think of these men and women living in Oregon or Florida, Maine or Arizona, in every state of the Union, creating from their own inner needs a record of a great country at peace. These are scenes of the harvest; these are a hundred different varieties of social comment; in this exhibition are pictured the activities which are characteristic of

III-10: *Adobe Workers, Ranchos de Taos Church*, pencil sketch, 9 x 12 inches, The University of Kansas Museum of Art, The Lockwood Collection

our country today. Also there are interpretations in color based on characters and events out of our past. It presents an American Saga. I for one am proud of it."[12]

The artists of this inclination, the illustrators of the American Saga, were related more by their sometimes flag-waving concern for native subjects than by a common style. Such concerns found expression in a variety of local schools — regionalisms — stretching from Provincetown to Seattle. The unique life and character of northern New Mexico was not immune to this; indeed, from the outset, Taos painters had stressed the local, the painting of the Spanish-American Scene.

III-11: *Adobe Workers, ca.* 1935, watercolor, 14 x 20 inches, Estate of the artist

Lockwood's sketches and easel pictures of the mid-thirties reflect this tendency. The theme of the adobe worker, certainly a Southwestern phenomenon, reappears in his work several times. His sketch of adobe workers at the Ranchos de Taos church (fig. III-10) has a quick, summary quality about it. More studied is his watercolor, *Adobe Workers*, done about 1935 (fig. III-11). Here again the figures echo the heavily contoured, angular poses of Boardman Robinson. The watercolor technique also has changed from its earlier Marin-like emphasis; the rapid, calligraphic line of the early 1930s watercolors is sacrificed for a more controlled, less spontaneous effect. In this Lockwood may be betraying the influence of the mural experience with its demand for large, generalized forms and areas of color.

Certainly a mural-like effect pervades Lockwood's major work of 1938, *The Corner Grocery (Cisneros Store)* (PLATE VII). As noted by one scholar, "*Corner Grocery Store*, with its ordered space, precise definition of form, and harmonious but variegated colors, demonstrates the influence of Lockwood's mural designs on his easel paintings."[13] Unlike some of the heavily impastoed canvases of a few years earlier, autographic brushwork in the 1938 work is much less evident; this may be due to the flat experience of working in fresco, which Lockwood used in several of his murals.

III-12: *Study for "The Corner Grocery," ca.* 1938, pencil, Archives of American Art, Smithsonian Institution

A comparison of the preliminary studies with the final painting is telling. The initial sketches of the saleswoman at the Cisneros store (fig. III-12), while scarcely portraiture, are considerably more specific than the series of spherical volumes to which her ample form is reduced in the final version. Similarly, a colored pencil study (fig. III-13) is characterized by a more individual touch than the final version. In the drawing the two customers at the counter, for instance, are individually clothed and distinguished from each other in pose and size; in the painting, all traces of uniqueness have been banished so that the figures appear to be cast from the same mold. Yet this tendency toward generalization is not inappropriate to the artist's intentions. The reliance on simplified and generalized elements within the composition ultimately yields an impression larger than the specific and more durable than the transient. *The Corner Grocery* becomes, as one critic has written, "a small monument to the commonplace dignity of everyday life."[14]

48

III-13: *Sketch for "The Corner Grocery," ca.* 1938, colored pencil,
17 x 22½ inches, University Art Museum, University of Texas,
Austin

Despite the acclaim accorded his murals from the 1930s, and the
resultant relative scarcity of easel work from the middle years of the
decade, it is clear that Lockwood continued to regard his easel painting
as being of importance. In October, 1937, Lockwood wrote enthusiastically of his return from murals to landscape painting: "I'm now
digging into some easel painting with vim — the country is beautiful . . . "[15] A few days later he wrote to another friend, repeating his
interest in the landscape and its depiction. Lockwood reported that
"Indian summer warms the valley here — it is so beautiful now that
any attempt to interpret it on canvas seems foolishly futile — too many
times I fear I am giving way to the pure physical enjoyment of it all,
but I console myself with the thought that that in itself is also one of
the ingredients of good painting."[16]

The pure physical enjoyments of easel painting ultimately brought
Lockwood back to that arena filled with new strength and determina-
tion. Thus it was that in response to Forbes Watson's request to publish
his murals, Lockwood wrote: " . . . I feel that reproduction of *only*
the mural photographs would omit what I consider to be an important
part of my work, easel painting, in which perhaps is more evident a
search for better things."[17]

49

# IV.   For the People: Lockwood Murals

**O**n February 7, 1933, Ward Lockwood complained in his journal that "The whole world seems to be caught in a mire of uncertainty and trouble for which no one has a solution. We are swayed by strange powers whose force is over-powering — However — ," continued the artist, "I'm sure this country needed something like this depression — a strong purge of some sort — to cure a land constipated by false values and poisoned by greed. Perhaps things will change for the better."[1]

Less than a month later, on March 4, Franklin Delano Roosevelt became the thirty-second president of the United States. On that date, nearly fifteen million Americans were unemployed, and of these close to ten thousand were artists. In the overall, bleak picture, the situation of these jobless artists may have seemed relatively insignificant; yet, as Francis O'Connor has noted, "the art they could produce was the first of the stricken nation's expendable luxuries. Artists were both unemployed and unemployable and the repute of the already established availed as little as the promise of youth. The blunt realities of the time demanded that an artist abandon his profession if he wanted to eat — or else accept the disgrace of the public dole."[2]

The Roosevelt inauguration and the birth of the New Deal gave hope that Lockwood's prophesy that "things will change for the better" would be realized. With speed and imagination, the Roosevelt administration moved to implement one of the most far-reaching programs of government support for the arts ever attempted.

Two months after his inauguration, Roosevelt received a letter from the painter George Biddle, who was a member of a prominent Philadelphia family, and a Groton and Harvard classmate of the President. Prompted by the dire economic situation of many of his fellow artists, and inspired by the heroic example of contemporary Mexican muralists, Biddle addressed his old schoolmate: "There is a matter which I have long considered and which someday might interest your administration . . . The younger artists of America are conscious that they have never been of the social revolution that our country and civilization are going through; and they would be very eager to express these ideals in a permanent art form if they were given the government's cooperation. They would be contributing to and expressing in living monuments the social ideals that you are struggling to achieve. And I am convinced that our mural art with a little impetus can soon result, for the first time in our history, in a vital national expression."[3]

Although artists had been on the state payroll in New York while Roosevelt was governor, Biddle was the first to gain the President's sympathetic attention to the idea that the federal government might similarly subsidize artists.[4] After confronting the bureaucratic tangle in Washington and the conservative resistance of the National Commission of Fine Arts, Biddle's baby was finally born as the Public Works of Art Project (PWAP) under the direction of Edward Bruce. The PWAP was an appendage of the Treasury Department, and with the later

Section of Fine Arts, (also administered through Treasury) and the Federal Art Program, it greatly affected American art and artists in the 1930s.

In the course of their ten-year existence, the federal art programs helped support painters and printmakers, sculptors and designers professionals and not-quite-professionals. Many of the innovators of the 1940s and 1950s, the heroes of the abstract expressionist movement, were alumni of the program, and in more than one case their professional lives were saved by the innovative Roosevelt experiment.

Although the abstract painters of the next decade may have been New Deal graduates, their government work and that of the other program artists in general was distinctly less innovative. Under Bruce's direction, the artists were directed to interpret the American scene. Edward B. Rowan, assistant director of the PWAP, announced that any artist who found only foreign subjects picturesque and deserving of attention "had better be dropped and an opportunity given to the man or woman with enough imagination and vision to use the beauty and possibility for aesthetic expression in the subject matter of his own country."[5] In establishing the Section of Fine Arts Bruce reiterated his allegiance to "the middle course," opposing both abstractionist "tripe" and classical "ladies in cheesecloth."[6] "Any artist who paints a nude for the Public Works of Art Project should have his head examined," declared the project leaders.[7] Bruce sought a representational, inoffensive art for the masses, which resulted in acres of American Scene murals and thousands of paintings and prints. As the Section chief admitted, he sought art that gave him "the same feeling I get when I smell a sound, fresh ear of corn."[8]

Today as well as during the 1930s the most apparent products of the Federal Art Project and Treasury Section are the murals painted for federal buildings, ranging from provincial post offices to governmental headquarters. Traditionally, Diego Rivera and other Mexican muralists, and their strong social statements, have been viewed as a key influence on the Americans. Edward Bruce, however, vowed to cope with their type of social protest in the Section commissions by halting the "Mexican invasion on the border."[9] Furthermore, the mural tradition was basically alien to the American artistic experience, and although the Mexicans' work may often have been regarded as an ideal, for most New Deal painters Rivera et al were not effective, working sources. Instead of social statements, those of the FAP and Section murals were large American Scene or American history paintings.

Among those Americans introduced to mural painting in this period was Ward Lockwood. Although he had in 1926 produced a "mural" for patrons at the Kansas City Country Club (fig. I-16), the commissions offered through the Roosevelt programs provided his first real opportunity to work in the large mural scale.

In 1932, the Taos County Court House was razed by fire. In the fall of the following year a new structure was erected, and its interior was decorated with ten murals done by four members of the local art colony under the auspices of the fledgling PWAP. The single largest mural was Victor Higgins' *Moses, the Law Giver.* The other artists and

51

IV-1: *Justice Begets Content*, 1933-34, fresco, approx. 84 x 36 inches,
Taos County Court House, Taos, New Mexico, photograph courtesy
Archives of American Art, Smithsonian Institution

their contributions were Emil Bisttram and his three murals, *Aspiration*, *Transgression*, and *Reconciliation*; Bert Phillips and his *Obedience Casts Out Fear* and *The Shadow of Crime*; and Lockwood, represented by four works, *Avarice Breeds Crime*, *Justice Begets Content*, *Superfluous Laws Oppress* and *Sufficient Law Protects*.

Unlike most of his subsequent murals, the subjects of Lockwood's Taos cycle are all non-specific; indeed, this lack of local themes, surprising in a place known for its specific views and subjects, is common to the entire Court House mural program. As explained by one source, "the compositions are allegorical because the historical events of Taos are yet subjects of bitter controversy."[10]

Although the appearance of Indian or Spanish-American figures in a multi-lingual, multi-cultural community like Taos is not unusual, it is not a customary subject for Lockwood to handle. However, his *Justice Begets Content* (fig. IV-1) uses the Indian subject common to the area, and the final work results from a series of studies of specific models (fig. IV-2). The mural's design is simple in its organization and somewhat stylized in its execution. The forms of face and figure are simplified and slightly angular, requirements forced upon the muralist by the necessity for his work to carry graphically over great distances. While Pueblo Indians modeled for *Justice Begets Content*, it was the artist's wife who posed for *Superfluous Laws Oppress* (figs. IV-3, 4). As with the *Justice* painting, the forms in the latter are large and simple. Both murals are organized around an emphatic diagonal rising from lower left to upper right.

The organization around diagonals is found as well in a third Lockwood mural from the 1933-34 project, *Avarice Breeds Crime* (fig. IV-5). In other respects, however, the *Avarice* mural, companion to *Justice Begets Content*, differs from the two Taos works previously considered. The narrow, vertical dimensions of the mural are given greater emphasis by the lowered vantage point, which causes the avaracious standing figure to loom over the other figures in the scene. The effect is like that of a cartoon or caricature enlarged to a grand scale, suggestive of a possible influence from Boardman Robinson.

IV-2: *Study for "Justice Begets Content,"* *ca.* 1933, charcoal, 18 x 12 inches, The University of Kansas Museum of Art, The Lockwood Collection

IV-4: *Study for "Superfluous Laws Oppress,"* *ca.* 1933, charcoal, 12 x 18 inches, The University of Kansas Museum of Art, The Lockwood Collection

IV-3: *Superfluous Laws Oppress*, 1933-34, fresco, approx. 84 x 60 inches, Taos County Court House, Taos, New Mexico, photograph courtesy Archives of American Art, Smithsonian Institution

IV-5: *Avarice Breeds Crime*, 1933-34, fresco, approx. 84 x 36 inches, Taos County Court House, Taos, New Mexico, photograph courtesy Archives of American Art, Smithsonian Institution

It was, in fact, in Colorado Springs, on Robinson's faculty, that Lockwood had made his first serious effort at mural painting. During the summer of 1933, while at the Broadmoor Art Academy, he executed an eight by twelve foot panel in true fresco, on an outside wall of one of the school's buildings. The structure and Lockwood's mural were razed about a year later to make way for the present Fine Arts Center. Although now destroyed, this first essay in fresco painting proved to be of great consequence for the artist. Lockwood undoubtedly received encouragement and advice from his friend, Robinson, who had been working with fresco for at least seven years. The Broadmoor attempt at fresco was successful enough that Lockwood used the medium again in his Taos Court House murals. As he later recalled, "I superintended the preparation of these [Taos] panels, the mixing of the plaster and did most of the plastering myself — so I thoroughly understand the procedure and the method. These murals are today [1936] in excellent condition and as far as I can discover have not changed a bit since the color dried."[11]

Fresco, which was used so effectively by the Mexican muralists of the period, enjoyed a revival in this country in the 1930s. The practice of fresco painting is an ancient and traditional one, "whose history goes back to the early memories of the race"; but its revival in modern times is more than another instance of revivalism. As noted by one of Lockwood's contemporaries, "our concern with fresco is by no means an archaeological reversion. We relearn the craft as a universal tool, particularly adaptable to the present social and aesthetic needs. Forces of which we only begin to be aware move us toward the collective activity and discussion that the fresco stimulates . . . In the very act of creating a fresco there is set up in miniature a model of the collective activity we need. Directors, architects, builders, masons, painters work for a common purpose. The painter, far from being concerned with the expression of his own personality, serves to coordinate and give form to the group ideas."[12] Fresco painting then was attractive to artists because it was a collective enterprise, which suggests a social or political justification, in place of an aesthetic one; because it offered a permanent integration of painted images with the architectural structures; because it provided the artists "a means of release from their introspective doubts and ineffectual lyricism" of easel painting;[13] and because, through reference to Old Master techniques and a lengthy tradition, it gave the artist a sense of historical justification.

Ward Lockwood's description of his work on the Taos County Court House frescoes was used as part of his argument to gain the Section's permission to do his Post Office Department murals in the same medium. The commissions for the decoration of the new Post Office Department headquarters were based on entries submitted to the Treasury Department's Section of Painting and Sculpture. The government made nearly $116,000 available for the twenty-two murals and fourteen sculpture commissions to decorate the Post Office and Treasury Department Buildings. The importance placed by the Section on this project was reflected in the anxiety with which American artists awaited the competition results in October, 1935. From Taos, Lockwood reported that "there will be quite a nervous tension in the art world around here for a few days after October 17th when the Washington

56

sketches are judged."[14] Among the commissions awarded for the Post Office Department Building was one to Ward Lockwood for two murals depicting the *Consolidation of the West* (figs. IV-6, 7).

These two large panels each measure six by thirteen and one-half feet, and were planned as a continuing unit, to "picture the history of the development of the West and Southwest from a time previous to the arrival of the Spanish Conquerors to the end of the Indian wars toward the end of the last century."[15] These murals, which rank as Lockwood's most ambitious and important works in the fresco medium, were originally intended to be done with oils on canvas. That plan was eventually set aside in favor of the fresco medium, in which Lockwood had earlier worked, and in which Reginald Marsh had previously executed one of the Post Office mural commissions. The decision to change the medium from oil to fresco took more than a year, and the commission, which was awarded in the fall of 1935, was not begun until 1937.[16] However, during this delay, the artist continued to work on his concept for the project.

Although some of the incidents were to vary, the overall design of the murals was remarkably consistent from the early sketches (figs. IV-8, 9) to the finished work. In a lengthy letter to the Section superintendent, Lockwood explained his working method and some of the changes that had occurred between the initial sketches and the final cartoons for the mural. "It is my habit of work in developing a mural," wrote Lockwood, "to keep the preliminary work in a malleable state while it is in the process of development. The design and drawing finally crystallize in the cartoon and the color and values in the final work."[17] Edward Rowan, responding for the Section, wrote: "Your habit of presenting preliminary work in a malleable state and finally crystallizing the design in the cartoon and the color and values in the final work is, in our estimation, the most intelligent procedure possible."[18]

Rowan's easy acceptance of the alterations in Lockwood's sketches was undoubtedly due in part to the fact that some of these changes were made in response to suggestions from the Section leaders. The Section defended its suggestions and instructions to artists — which were not infrequent — on the grounds that "in the final analysis, the members of the Section will be responsible for the work that goes up."[19] The artist's agreement to such suggestions was probably based on their awareness that the work's acceptance by the Section preceded payment. In approving Lockwood's request to change from oil to fresco, one Section consultant made it clear that he consented only "if this is not an excuse for too sloppy technique and drawing." Then he added, the "drawing of the horse [is] very weak."[20] As if in response to such criticism, Lockwood noted that the design only crystallized in the cartoons, where he "attempted to make the abstract design and the aesthetic elements as fine as possible."[21] In the cartoon Lockwood felt that the horse and Pony Express rider, earlier the butt of Section criticism, had been "brought . . . into the design in a more acceptable manner."[22]

Other changes in Lockwood's scheme are explained not by Section decree but by the extensive research which the artist conducted in the

57

IV-6: *Consolidation of the West*, 1937, fresco, 72 by 162 inches, Post
Office Department Building, Washington, D. C., photograph
courtesy Public Buildings Service, National Archives (121-PS-9476)

IV-8: *Study for the Post Office Murals*, ca. 1935, location unknown,
photograph courtesy Public Buildings Service, National Archives
(121-PS-149)

IV-7: *Consolidation of the West*, 1937, fresco, 72 x 162 inches, Post Office Department Building, Washington, D. C., photograph courtesy Public Buildings Service, National Archives (121-PS-9474)

IV-9: *Study for the Post Office Murals, ca.* 1935, location unknown, photograph courtesy Public Buildings Service, National Archives (121-PS-148)

IV-10:
*Costume Studies for Post Office Murals*, ca.1935-37, pencil, 12 x 9 inches, The University of Kansas Museum of Art,
The Lockwood Collection

IV-11:
Photograph of model in period costume, Estate of the artist

preparation of his work. The tendency by Depression era writers and artists to turn backward in quest of a usable American past has often been noted.[23] Reacting to the insecurity of their own times, the creative minds of the 1930s frequently sought answers in the lessons of history. "We need to know," wrote John Dos Passos, "what kind of firm ground other men, belonging to generations before us, have found to stand on."[24] A strong tendency toward historicism grew with the period. As one observer has noted, "meticulous attention to authenticity became a canon of the decade."[25] Sometimes the details came to be of greater importance than the whole.

Lockwood, like other artists of the period, was clearly a part of this tendency toward historicism. Submitting his cartoons for the Post Office murals to the Section of Painting and Sculpture, he proudly noted that "everything in the designs is authenticated by authoritative research, from the number of spokes in the rear wheel of a stage coach to the number of buttons on a major general's coat in the year 1877."[26] The obsession with detail and historical accuracy is seen in Lockwood's notebooks for the mural project, which are filled with period costume studies (fig. IV-10), verbal descriptions of wagons and vehicles, photographs of antique armor (fig. IV-11) and the like, all of which served in the preparation of his final cartoons and completed mural.

In the process of the image's crystallization changes were also made based on the artist's own artistic decisions. Lockwood for instance, felt that the log houses being built in the initial sketches were too commonly found in the work of the government muralists; hence, in the final version the log house is replaced by an adobe structure which is more unusual, and therefore perhaps more interesting. However, as Lockwood carefully pointed out to the Section, the new adobe house "factually is equally as authentic" in the Southwest.[28]

The mother and child — Lockwood's "Madonna of the plains"[29] — have been moved from the pioneer group on the left to the home-building group on the right, a transition which the artist felt made better aesthetic and domestic sense. For reasons which similarly combine common sense with artistic decisions, Lockwood deleted the incident of Indian atrocity on the right panel from the final mural (see fig. IV-9). "[T]he emotional effect [of this incident] was incongruous being placed so near the figures of the home builders. Also, the incident is distinctly a subject that is controversial. As a matter of fact, after research, I have concluded that the Americans perhaps committed worse atrocities than the Indians."[30]

The various figures and details within the final composition were drawn from a number of sources, including photographs, book illustrations, sketches of Indian ceremonials, and studies from the live model. In the autumn of 1931, the Lockwoods traveled to the Hopi villages of northern New Mexico and there witnessed the fascinating tribal snake dance, a ceremony which has caught the attention of many New Mexico artists (fig. IV-12). In his journal Lockwood exclaimed: " . . . the barbaric stark beauty of the figures in the dance was a revelation — no ordinary tourist sideshow this! The spectacle is burned in my memory!"[31] Lockwood's early sketches (figs. IV-13, 14) evince an ethnographic and herpetological concern that is somewhat diminished in

IV-12: Joseph Imhof, *Snake Dance*, watercolor,
Museum of New Mexico, Santa Fe

IV-13: *Hopi Snake Dancer*, watercolor,
Archives of American Art,
Smithsonian Institution

the final powerful but more abstract figure in the Post Office Building lobby. In his studies of the snake, the artist used book illustrations which he taped into his sketchbook, and went so far as to obtain a rubbing of the rattler's skin in order to understand exactly the character of its scaly texture (see fig. IV-14).

The artist freely resorted to the camera as a means of preparing studies, as with the figure of the prospector in the left panel. Here the final version relies upon drawings (fig. IV-15) made from photographs of the same subject (fig. IV-16). Similarly, passages within the background landscape are remarkably close to illustrations which Lockwood clipped from magazines, and the Conestoga wagon in the background was also inspired by study from photographs and illustrations.

By far the most sensitive studies, however, are those which were done directly in Lockwood's studio from the live model. In drawings for the Indian at the far left (fig. IV-18) or the military officer at the right (fig. IV-17) we find Lockwood's draughtsmanship at its best, responding to the real problem of the human presence, rather than to the abstract notion of conquistadore or Pony Express rider or to the substitute presence of the photograph.

The final cartoons for the mural were ready by March, 1937, and Lockwood did the actual work on the Post Office frescoes during the following summer. The *Consolidation of the West* generated considerable favorable comment, but by no means was this unanimous. Edward Alden Jewell, reviewing the Post Office project for the *New York Times*, found that "Lockwood's scheme is hard, angular and somewhat bleak, as contrasted with the softer, more gently rounded form created by Mr. [Frank] Mechau" in a neighboring part of the building.[32] On the contrary, Raoul Dufy, visiting Washington to

IV-14: Notebook pages with studies of rattlesnakes, *ca.* 1935-37, mixed media, each page 12 x 9 inches, The University of Kansas Museum of Art, The Lockwood Collection

IV-15: *Study of a Burro for Post Office Murals*,
   *ca.* 1935-37, charcoal, 15 x 20 inches,
   The University of Kansas Museum of Art,
   The Lockwood Collection

IV-16: Photograph of pack burro,
   Estate of the artist

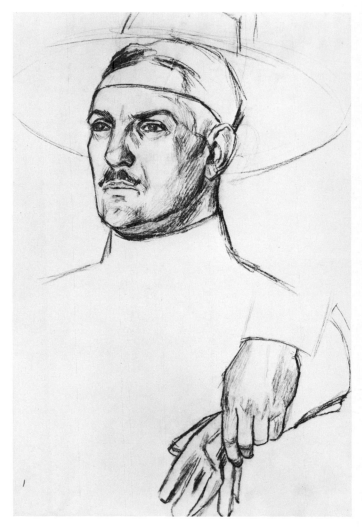

IV-17: *Figure Study for Post Office Murals*,
   *ca.* 1935-37, charcoal, 20½ x 13¾ inches,
   The University of Kansas Museum of Art,
   The Lockwood Collection

study the New Deal art projects as a possible prototype for the French government, was greatly impressed with the mural and "considered Lockwood an exceptionally brilliant exponent of fresco."[33] Forbes Watson considered the *Consolidation of the West* to be "one of the most beautiful in its rich colors of any of our murals."[34] Edward Rowan felt that Lockwood's Post Office mural was "holding up beautifully. It is clear, clean and honest and is altogether a sincere achievement."[35] In the game of New Deal aesthetics, it was not what the *Times'* critics nor Parisian painters thought that counted; rather, the acclaim of Section administrators was all-important, and this Lockwood was fortunate to gather frequently.

The Washington frescoes are similar in format and western subject to the *Pioneers in Kansas* mural for the Wichita Post Office, which Lockwood executed in 1935. The relationship between these two commissions is understandable for Lockwood was working on the Wichita design at the same time he was completing sketches for the Post Office Department competition. Like the later Washington frescoes, the Wichita project was awarded through the Section of Painting and Sculpture in open competition. Eighty-one sketches by forty-one artists were submitted, from which the local Kansas committee selected forty designs; these in turn were forwarded to Edward Rowan for final selection and awarding of contracts. Lockwood and Richard Haines were awarded the two commissions on the basis of their entries (figs. IV-19, 20).

IV-18: *Figure Study for Post Office Murals, ca.* 1935-37, brown conte crayon, 15¼ x 21¼ inches, The University of Kansas Museum of Art, The Lockwood Collection

In the initial screening the Kansas State Federation of Art "endeavored to be very liberal in our selection of the group for [the Section's] final consideration." The forty designs forwarded to Rowan were sent with little comment. The committee had basically but "one thing that we are especially concerned about, and that is that nothing appear in any of the finished designs that will in any way glorify the ill treatment the Indian has received in the hands of the white man. We mention this simply because in one or two instances there is evidence of this."[16] One of those instances was Lockwood's entry, in which an Indian cowers in the foreground, fearful of the Pony Express rider who seems about to run him down. After the commissions had been awarded, C. A. Seward, director of the Kansas State Federation of Art, wrote the artist with suggestions which "in no way are intended as 'orders' to change your design in general arrangements, etc., but merely to avoid as little public criticism as possible after the murals are in place." As he had done earlier to Rowan, Seward repeated to Lockwood his concern over the crouching Indian in the foreground. "If you can do something with him to eliminate the suggestion of the ruthless dominance of the white man," Seward suggested, "it would seem to us to be better." He explained that the Indian in Kansas received better treatment than elsewhere, "and while we are not proud of our record in general, yet we would rather not recall the unpleasantness of the suggestion. Could you change the 'scared Indian' to one taking an active part in the means of communication — show him giving a hailing sign, a friendly sign or a smoke signal?" These suggestions the director ventured "as a result of our own reaction and the supporting reaction of the public."[37]

Never one to flout his patron's wishes, Lockwood revised his sketches to eliminate any suggestion of ruthless dominance of the white man. Seward and his public, however, could scarcely have counted on the overcompensation which Lockwood made. In the final scheme the Indian no longer cowers, but neither does he offer Seward's friendly sign or smoke signal; instead, he reverses the situation, and the Indian now confronts the rider through the deadly sights of his long rifle (fig. IV-21).

With the exception of the startling reversal in the relationship of rider to Indian, all other changes in the crystallization from competition sketch to finished mural (fig. IV-22) were minor, and none of them greatly affected the original conception. Like the Washington murals, the details in *Pioneers in Kansas* were the result of extensive technical research by the artist involving period costumes, construction of stage coaches, and the like. Unlike the Post Office Department frescoes, however, the Wichita murals were executed with oils on canvas, using the best mural linen available and "the highest grade of artist's colors — not so-called 'decorator's colors'."[38] The mural, painted in Taos, was installed in Wichita shortly after Christmas, 1935, by which time Lockwood had already begun the lengthy work on the Washington project.

The completion of the Post Office Department murals was delayed not only by the indecision regarding medium, but also by Lockwood's work in 1936 on a private mural commission for the Colorado Springs

IV-19: *Original Sketch for Wichita Post Office Mural*, 1935, location
unknown, photograph courtesy Public Buildings Service, National
Archives (121-PS-9479)

IV-20: Richard Haines, *Original Sketch for Wichita Post Office Mural*,
1935, location unknown, photograph courtesy Lockwood Estate

IV-21: *Study for Wichita Post Office Mural*, 1935, ink wash, 9 x
21⅛ inches, The University of Kansas Museum of Art, The Lockwood Collection

IV-22: *Pioneers in Kansas*, 1935, oil on canvas, Wichita Post Office,
Wichita, Kansas, photograph courtesy Public Buildings Service,
National Archives (121-PS-182)

IV-23: Kenneth Adams, *Ballet Mural*,
1936, oil on canvas,
Colorado Springs Fine Arts Center

Fine Arts Center. Constructed on the site of Lockwood's first fresco effort, the new Art Center was the pride of the region, and following its completion in 1935 mural commissions were awarded to Boardman Robinson, Andrew Dasburg, Kenneth Adams and Ward Lockwood. The last three artists were given the murals in the lounge for the Art Center's theater, and their four panels are all related to the performing arts. Adams' decorative mural, *Ballet* (fig. IV-23), was the first completed, and it was characterized by the abbreviated, schematic handling of the human form which was found with increasing frequency in his work from the mid-thirties onward.

The flat, abstract patterning, typical of Art Deco design, was also adapted by Lockwood in his panels based upon the American theater (fig. IV-24). The subjects and execution are remarkably different from Lockwood's murals which immediately preceded and followed this commission, and this change seems due in part to the influence exhibited by his friends Adams and Dasburg (see fig. IV-25). The left panel (fig. IV-26) represents figures from *Uncle Tom's Cabin*, *The Girl of the Golden West* and *Rip Van Winkle* which, according to the artist, were "three of the outstanding plays which are purely American."[39] These theatrical figures are accompanied in the right-hand panel by an American minstrel performer, a light opera singer and Charlie Chaplin, representing the cinema.

In each mural, the separate figures are compartmentalized and unity in design is achieved through a common palette and through abstract forms which weave among the figures and tie them together. These patterned shapes not only relate the parts of the "triptych" to each other; they also add to the light decorative quality of the composition. Lockwood said: "I have attempted to achieve in these murals a flower-like quality to relieve the rigidity of straight vertical and horizontal lines inherent in the functional design of the architecture. At the same time an attempt has been made to preserve the neatness and precision that one feels when in the lounge . . . On the whole I have tried to make the murals in color and in design an integral part of the building as the skin is a part of the human body."[40]

IV-25: Andrew Dasburg, *Circus Mural*, *ca.* 1936, oil on canvas,
Colorado Springs Fine Arts Center

IV-24: Theater Lounge, Colorado Springs Fine Arts Center, with Ward
Lockwood's murals

IV-26: *The American Theater Mural*, 1936, oil on canvas, Colorado
Springs Fine Arts Center

Although Lockwood's success in the government's mural programs brought occasional private commissions, such as that at Colorado Springs, mural patronage remained primarily the government's domain throughout the 1930s. Following upon the good reception of his efforts for the Section in Wichita and Washington, Lockwood was invited in 1937 to enter a design for the mural decoration of the Post Office and Court House in Lexington, Kentucky. After receiving the request from Rowan, "thoroughbreds, Daniel Boones and Henry Clays, etc., . . . kaleidoscoped through [Lockwood's] head . . ."[41] Lockwood considered a wide range of subjects for his design, including allegory, contemporary scenes, and local history, but "finally decided on a historical theme because, everything considered, I believe that it will be the most satisfactory from the viewpoint of the Section, the people of Lexington and myself."[42]

The particular incident selected was Daniel Boone's arrival in Kentucky in the spring of 1769 (fig. IV-27). Like the period's ubiquitous *Young Mr. Lincoln*, like John Steuart Curry's or Stephen Vincent Benet's John Brown, and like a host of other newly-resurrected folk heroes and national leaders, Lockwood's Boone symbolizes a national ideal as representative of the American people, the common folk. As noted by one scholar, "the nationalism of the ['30s] decade stimulated an emphasis upon the uniqueness of American ideas and values" which could be embodied by the rugged individualist Daniel Boone. "In many ways, American writers [and artists] turned their backs on the Old World. Not the seaboard nation of small-clothes, trans-atlantic citizens and 'Good Feelings' attracted them, but the interior country with its homespun garb, provincial politics and sectional animosities. The pioneer farmer much more than the merchant trader represented the American character for these twentieth-century citizens."[43]

The moment depicted by Lockwood was enthusiastically described by a member of the Lexington press. "From a knoll," he reported, "Boone and his five companions view the rolling land. Here indeed was a 'promised land,' teeming with all sorts of wild game, abounding in verdure and fertile byond their hope and imaginations. At the pictorial moment, the explorers are a month away from home. They have trudged over almost impassable mountains, blazing a trail through a strange country, avoiding the Indians, constantly facing unknown dangers. Then, the sight of the lands before them make bright with wonder and discovery the weary faces of the adventurers." The journalistic excesses of this report make it sound more like a description of a theatrical spectacle than a static mural; but the writer concludes that "it is the spirit of this event that the artist has attempted to capture."[44]

In fact, Lockwood's mural is considerably more restrained than the newspaper description of it. The faces "bright with wonder" are rather solemn, a fact which Rowan noted in viewing the cartoon for the mural (fig. IV-28). He wrote that the cartoon was "replete with handsome drawing on which I congratulate you." Rowan did, however, take the opportunity to offer the Section's suggestion "that the expression of the faces seem to some of us to be overly austere.

IV-27: *Daniel Boone Discovering Kentucky*, 1937, oil on canvas, 138 x
96 inches, Post Office and Court House Building, Lexington,
Kentucky, photograph courtesy Public Buildings Service, National
Archives (121-PS-2131)

IV-28: *Cartoon for the Lexington Post Office Mural*, 1937,
location unknown, photograph courtesy Public
Buildings Service, National Archives (121-PS-4566)

IV-29: *Study for the Lexington Post Office Mural*, 1937,
brown conte crayon, 26 x 18½ inches,
The University of Kansas Museum of Art,
The Lockwood Collection

IV-30: *Sketch for Lexington Post Office Mural,*
1937, tempera on board, 24 x 16¼ inches,
The University of Kansas Museum of Art,
The Lockwood Collection

IV-31: *Study for the Lexington Post Office, Mural,*
1937, location unknown, photograph courtesy
Public Buildings Service, National Archives
(121-PS-1542)

One wonders if Boone at the moment of his great realization which you
depict would not have worn a more enlightened expression."[45] Lockwood apparently felt not, for the only significant change from cartoon
to canvas is in the kneeling foreground figure, in which the youthful
model, Hayes Lyon (fig. IV-29), has been replaced by an older,
bearded man.

On behalf of the Section, Rowan also offered criticism of Lockwood's color sketches (fig. IV-30), saying that they had lost the
"robust quality" of the black and white studies (fig. IV-31). Henry
Varnum Poor thought that "the color was in every way distinguished,"
but another Section committee member "felt that the general tonality
was slightly too bland." The Committee felt that "the blue greens are
rather insistent" and should not be increased in the final work, and
they agreed that "if you achieve the feeling of air around your figures
and around the trees that more conviction would be given to the place-
ment of the figures in the group."[46]

IV-32: *Sketch for the Lexington Post Office Mural*, 1937, pencil, The Archives of American Art, Smithsonian Institution

Lockwood took the section's criticism in stride, perhaps being accustomed to such by that time. He duly thanked Rowan for his suggestions, noting that "I was aware of these defects in the color sketch myself and am glad that the self-criticism is corroborated."[47] Indeed, in the final work the mannered elongations and "strident color" of the sketch are deleted, and the "robust quality" reappears.

Lockwood was attracted to Boone not only for his local affiliations, but also because he helped frame Kentucky's first laws and was appointed a syndic or judge; hence, the subject was particularly appropriate to the court room setting for which the mural was destined. Compositionally Lockwood also sought to make the painting accord with its setting. He noted that "verticals predominate in the design of the sketch and give it, I think, a dignity which will fit in the court room."[48] From the outset the design had been marked by a pronounced verticality (see fig. IV-32); but this severe elongation of form and distortion of figure were mitigated in the final version, and nearly photographic likenesses of the figures resulted. In this Lockwood neatly satisfied the Section's predilection for an art that was representational, public and *American*. Rowan commented on the "distinguished quality of the work,"[49] and regarded the Lexington mural "as one of the fine American expressions of the past few years . . . "[50] He also reported that "Forbes [Watson] thinks it may be the finest thing we have done to date."[51]

The Lexington commission, which generated the highest praise from Section officials, was to be Lockwood's last major contract with the government. As noted earlier, he was by the late 1930s anxious to regain time lost from his easel painting. In 1938 Lockwood accepted a teaching post in Texas which, in addition to occupying the majority of his time, alleviated the need for financial support through mural commissions. In 1939, he did receive a commission for the murals in the post office at Edinburg, Texas. For this agricultural town in the fertile Rio Grande Valley, Lockwood selected a local subject, the open-air fruit stands which abound in the area

IV-33: *Color Sketch for Edinburg, Texas, Post Office Mural, ca.* 1939,
location unknown, photograph courtesy Public Buildings Service,
National Archives (121-PS-9480)

IV-34: *Sketch for Edinburg, Texas, Post Office Mural, ca.* 1939,
location unknown, photograph courtesy Public Buildings Service,
National Archives (121-PS-9482)

(fig. IV-33). The mural design was based upon Lockwood's own
sketches of the region, and in both its preliminary studies (fig. IV-34)
and final form it relates strongly to his earlier Taos painting of *The
Corner Grocery (Cisneros Store)* (fig. III-15). The decorative patterning of stacked produce, and the schematic flattening of form are
common to both the murals and the easel painting.

In October, 1938, the Section of Painting and Sculpture had been
renamed the Section of Fine Arts. During the preceding summer
Congressional opponents of the Roosevelt administration's social
programs had rallied, and the New Deal cultural programs were
among their first targets. It was charged that they were radical and
corrupt. Concurrently, in Europe, Hitler's Third Reich began to
threaten the tenuous balance of power which had persisted for a
decade; the Continent and ultimately the United States began to slip
inexorably toward war.

IV-35: *Sketch for Hamilton, Texas, Post Office Mural, ca.* 1941,
location unknown, photograph courtesy Public Buildings Service,
National Archives (121-PS-9484)

In 1941, on the eve of American entrance into the Second World War,
Lockwood was awarded his last government commission, for the post
office at Hamilton, Texas. As at Edinburg, he selected a local theme,
Texas Rangers relaxing in camp (fig. IV-35). "By this time," he
observed, "I am pretty well acquainted with the sentiment and sentimentality of the Texans and feel certain they will like such a mural."[52]
Indeed, Lockwood's appraisal of his audience seems to have been rather
accurate. Upon the unveiling of the work the local newspaper
reported that "Every Hamiltonian and every Texan who's ever read a
book, seen a movie or listened to the tales their grandfathers told can
appreciate *Texas Rangers in Camp.*" Then, no doubt intending the
highest compliment, the journalist enthusiastically concluded that
"even a Texas Ranger himself could appreciate Lockwood's art!"[53]

The work on the mural required more time than the artist had
planned, and he was forced to request extensions from the Section.
The Hamilton project was not completed until May, 1942, barely a
year before the final phasing out, by Presidential decree, of all New
Deal art projects. Born of economic despair and necessity in 1933, the
programs flourished for a decade before dying of economic despair
and renewed warfare in mid-1943. Toward the end, Ward Lockwood
found himself in the curious and difficult position of designing a
decorative mural based on local folk heroes for a provincial post office,
while at the same time teaching camouflage techniques in a university
art curriculum geared toward the efforts of international warfare. It
was an intolerable situation in which finally the murals — and the
government art programs of the 1930s — had to give way.

# V. Austin: A University Experiment

In June, 1938, Lockwood supervised the installation of his Daniel Boone mural in Lexington, one of his last projects for the government. "Although from a financial angle these commissions were most welcome," Lockwood wrote, "they did consume much time and checked the production of easel painting to a much greater extent than I had desired."[1] The completion of mural projects in Wichita, Washington, Colorado Springs and Lexington, all within the span of three years, made Lockwood especially anxious for a leisurely return to his studio and his easel painting. It was at that time, however, that he was unexpectedly invited to join the faculty at the University of Texas. He was offered an appointment as professor of art, with the challenge of organizing an art department in an entirely new College of Fine Arts. In later recalling his decision, Lockwood was "surprised not only by the offer but by my acceptance of it, for to become a professor of a university was an event completely foreign to any dream, wish or plan I ever had . . . I thought: 'I'll try this job for a few years and then return to Taos' — but this move turned out to follow a wide curve in the road, the end of which we could not see."[2]

During the summer of 1938 Lockwood moved from Taos to Austin, leaving behind him the surroundings which had nurtured his art for more than a decade. During that period the art colony had changed considerably. In 1935 Andrew Dasburg, from whom Lockwood had derived guidance and inspiration, was stricken with Addison's disease which was to interrupt his painting career for eleven years. The deaths in 1936 of Irving Couse and Herbert Dunton deprived the colony of two of its leading "oldtimers," both of whom had been charter members of the Taos Society of Artists. In 1938, the same year as Lockwood's departure, Kenneth Adams also accepted a faculty position at the University of New Mexico in Albuquerque. The Taos fraternity which had sustained Lockwood and his artistic brethren began to wane in the late 1930s, a decline that was accelerated about 1940 and finally completed by renewed international conflict. One writer who was familiar with Taos noted that "World War II abruptly ended the period. With the great influx of new residents, the beauty of the valley, the slow tempo of the Spanish-American village, and the rhythmic appeal of pueblo life have given way to the ruthless demands of economic development and commercial exploitation. Art is no longer paramount. The supermarket, the filling station, the travel folder and highway billboard advertise Taos as no different than any other spot in America. Its successful sales exploiter today sit [sic] at the head of the table, while the artists wait for second helpings of public esteem."[3]

Although living in Austin, the Lockwoods continued to consider New Mexico as home, even through its wartime and postwar periods of transition. In 1940 they sold their original home and subsequently acquired the house at Talpa which they continued to own until their deaths. While remaining a Taoseno at heart, Ward Lockwood readily adapted to his new Texas environment. The landscape offered new pictorial possibilities, such as the Houston docks (fig. V-1). The classroom also offered new possibilities and new challenges. In his work, Lockwood saw himself and his generation as participants in an artistic revolution with a history dating back to the early years of the century. "In large measure," he wrote, "it is a revolt against the mechanical standardization of our society. It is an effort to limit the flood of machine-made materials and objects which threaten to engulf us — a reaction against the deadening duplication of millions of things our bored eyes encounter daily."[4] It was the revolution he sought to carry with him into the classroom.

Confirmed in his allegiance to nature as inspiration for his art, Lockwood during his early university years continued his primary interest in landscape painting. The summers free from classroom obligations permitted him to travel throughout the West, not only to Taos. Although New Mexico remained his home and favorite retreat, Lockwood also journeyed with some frequency to Colorado, and westward to the California coast. His view of Bryce Canyon (fig. V-2) shows his tendency to seek out and develop the abstract designs contained within the landscape scene. Instead of the panoramic sweep of the Taos "valleyscapes," this Utah watercolor arranges the rocky forms in a jewellike pattern across the surface of the paper, stressing the design potential of these curious forms.

Conditioned by his familiarity with the spectacular Taos Valley, Lockwood was apparently drawn to the unusual and the grand in the western landscapes, such as Bryce Canyon. Recalling a 1937 motor trip to California, he wrote: "Saw many of the 'biggest' in the world on the

V-1: *Harbor, Houston Docks*, oil on masonite, 18 x 24 inches, Estate of the artist

V-2: *Bryce Canyon, Utah,* 1939, watercolor, 13½ x 19½ inches, The
University of Kansas Museum of Art, The Lockwood Collection

V-3: *Horses in Winter, ca.* 1940, watercolor, 13¾ x 19¼ inches, The
Phillips Collection, Washington, D. C.

trip — the biggest ocean, the biggest two bridges, the biggest dam
(Boulder), the biggest canyon, the biggest meteor hole in the earth — all
of which were very impressive — especially when compared to the
smallness of the one ounce jiggers used at practically all of the bars."[5]

It continued, however, to be Taos and the New Mexican landscape
that had the strongest power over Lockwood. There, in John Marin's
terms, he could "re-true" himself. His watercolor of *Horses in
Winter* (fig. V-3), done about 1940, shows the continuation of his
mastery in that medium, especially as applied to the familiar Taos
landscape. At other times, the form of animal and landscape were
handled with a conscious but curious naivete, as if drawn by a child;
but the dislocations of form and space in *Landscape with Horses* (fig.
V-4) grow logically out of the angular distortions of his earlier
watercolor technique. Throughout the remainder of his career, this
motif of valley and horses continued to be a favorite of Ward Lockwood's (see fig. V-5).

80

V-4: *Landscape with Horses*, oil on canvas, 29¾ x 40 inches, The
Anshutz Collection, Denver

V-5: *Ranchito*, 1957, conte crayon, 22 x 31 inches, Estate of the artist

V-6: *Study for "Siesta,"* pencil, 9 x 12 inches, The University of Kansas Museum of Art, The Lockwood Collection

V-7: *Adobe Walls*, lithograph, 10¼ x 13½ inches, The University of Kansas Museum of Art, The Lockwood Collection

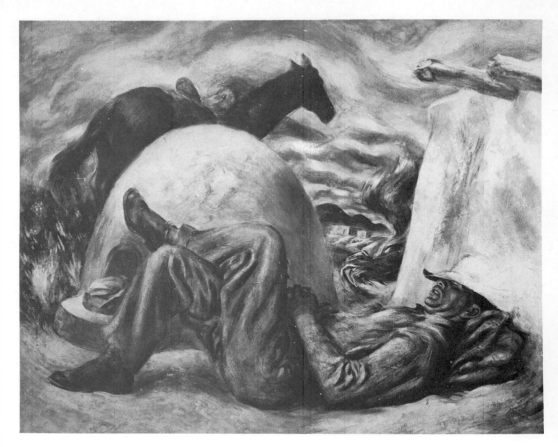

V-8: *Siesta, ca.* 1940, oil on masonite, 26¼ x 32¾ inches, Estate of the artist

V-9: *Study for "Siesta," ca.* 1940, pencil,
    Archives of American Art, Smithsonian Institution

V-10: *Siesta*, 1940, oil on masonite, 28 x 38 inches, The University
of Kansas Museum of Art, The Lockwood Collection

The people of Taos, as well as the New Mexican landscape, continued to interest Lockwood during his summer sojourns there. *The Corner Grocery* of 1938 (PLATE VII) is perhaps the best known of his Taos genre paintings, but by no means is it the only one. In 1940, Lockwood produced a series of works relating to the theme of the siesta. The preliminary sketchbook notations (fig. V-6) served as the basis for subsequent lithographs (fig. V-7) and also contained the germ of a concept which was to be realized in two final versions of *The Siesta*. The smaller of these two paintings (fig. V-8) includes details of adobe architecture and horse, which also appear in the sketchbooks (fig. V-9). As with *The Corner Grocery*, the forms are large and rhythmic, though handled with greater particularization than the earlier work. However, in varying degrees, both paintings show the impact of the mural experience and its requisite large, simple forms upon the easel painter.

The tendency toward bold formal design in the first version of *The Siesta* is further strengthened in the second painting of this theme (fig. V-10). The details of horse and architecture which made the focus diffuse in the earlier painting are here eliminated; in their place, the rounded form behind the reclining figure has been made higher and more prominent, as a foil to the curving contours of the sleeping man. The treatment of sky and distant landscape are more simplified, placing the attention on the repeated pattern of rounded forms rather than on particular details. That this subject held a continuing appeal for the artist is indicated by his return to it several times later in his life.

*Siesta*, done with oil glazes over egg tempera, not only showed a strong formal and compositional concern, but also betrayed Lockwood's increased interest in experimental techniques and new materials.[6] Throughout the preceding decade, many American painters had shown a keen interest in the techniques of the Old Masters, which accounted in part for the revival of painting in egg tempera, true fresco and the like. This study of historical techniques and materials also led to the development of new approaches. Among the latter was Lockwood's use of a waxed watercolor technique. As he explained in a 1941 manuscript on "A New Way to Paint with Watercolor," his experiments with this method began in the mid-1930s. "They grew out of my desire to make watercolor behave more like true fresco in which medium a pure white reflective surface underlies coats of transparent and translucent color which are super-imposed a few minutes apart without disturbing the tones underneath." Lockwood's procedure involved two operations. "First the use of gelatin glue hardened with a formalin solution which will allow numerous coats of transparent watercolor to be super-imposed over a fine white ground; second, the waxing of the finished surface to seal the pigment from the atmosphere and to make the watercolor waterproof."[7] Lockwood argued that a painting produced in this way would have "more 'depth' and life than the ordinary watercolor because the reflective power of the ground has been increased and the dark-light range is lengthened. Darks should be more luminous, lights more brilliant."[8] The artist also wrote that his system would make the watercolor medium "infinitely pliable and capable of revision," which would produce "a finer result than the

V-11: *Kiowa Indian Dancing, ca.* 1940,
gouache on paper, 29¼ x 20½ inches,
Estate of the artist

usual way."[9] And, finally, Lockwood's waxed watercolors had the advantage of not requiring glazing.

Although Lockwood apparently invested considerable time and thought in the development of his system and the manuscript explaining it, there are relatively few finished works done in this medium. Among the most ambitious is his *Kiowa Indian Dance* of 1940 (PLATE VIII). That the watercolor has survived the passage of time unglazed and undamaged attests to the durability of the wax technique. As noteworthy as the medium is the new strength of Lockwood's stylization evidenced by this work. The animated forms of the Indian dancers are rendered with a rapid, staccato line, which echoes the beat of the dance itself. The zigzag lines and angular forms center on a feathered pattern which establishes the rhythm within the composition. In its active design and schematized anatomy, Lockwood's *Kiowa Indian Dance* marks a departure from the studied approach to the Indian found in his mural sketches (see fig. IV-13). As design considerations replaced those of ethnographic exactness, the forms of Lockwood's Indians became less substantial and surface patterns became more predominant (fig. V-11). The centrifugal arrangement of abbreviated, jagged forms in *Kiowa Indian Dance* represents a culmination of this tendency.

86

The novelty of the Kiowa watercolor was not found in all his works of the period. In 1941 the Lockwoods spent some of their summer in Colorado, where the artist continued to explore many of the same landscape problems he had confronted during the preceding decade in Taos. In the picturesque mining town of Ouray, where he passed a portion of his holiday, Lockwood sketched the main street against its mountainous backdrop (fig. V-12). Unlike most of his earlier landscape drawings, but similar to his mural sketches, Lockwood made extensive verbal notations in the drawing, primarily regarding color and patterns. The quick sketches and verbal notes then were used as the basis for watercolors which were completed in his studio (fig. V-13).

V-12: *Sketch of Ouray, Colorado*, 1941, pencil, Archives of American Art, Smithsonian Institution

V-13: *Mining Town*, 1941, watercolor, 15 x 21 inches, Estate of the artist

V-14: *Stage Design for "Marco Millions," I:4*, 1939, watercolor,
Drama Department, University of Texas, Austin

The university affiliation which Lockwood established in 1938 brought new opportunities and new challenges to the artist. Primary among these, of course, was the formation of the new art department, and the instruction of aspiring students. At the end of his career, Lockwood reflected on the lot of the artist-teacher. He felt that such a situation provided "a rewarding and enriching life to an extent beyond the comprehension of those who have not experienced it." Not only did the university base keep Lockwood "constantly associated with youth," but it also brought stimulating contact with other artists, and with men and women "in other fields of high endeavor — in music, drama, literature, science."[10] Such acquaintanceships sometimes led Lockwood into new areas, such as theater set design. During his first year at the Austin campus, he was asked to do the scene designs for Eugene O'Neill's *Marco Millions* (fig. V-14). Aside from a generally decorative quality, which might relate to some of his mural projects, these set designs show little similarity to the rest of Lockwood's *oeuvre*.

Later, university contacts also brought Lockwood the chance to renew his work as an illustrator, when he was asked to provide the illustrations for Roy Bedichek's *Adventures with a Texas Naturalist*. While some of Lockwood's drawings for the book are in a rather realistic, documentary vein, most are more fanciful (fig. V-15). In this they again show affinities with earlier mural designs (fig. V-16). Although neither the set designs nor the illustrations are central to his work of the period, both show the variety of intellectual and artistic stimuli which Lockwood discovered in the university community; and it was in academia that Lockwood was to remain for most of his career.

V-15: Illustration from "Adventures with a Texas Naturalist"

V-16: Competition Study for Justice Department Building Murals, detail, location unknown, photograph courtesy Public Buildings Service, National Archives (121-MSW-43-165)

# VI. Berkeley: Process and Instruction

VI-1:
*Self-portrait, ca.* 1941, pencil,
Archives of American Art,
Smithsonian Institution

VI-2:
*Soldier*, 1945, oil on masonite,
20 x 16 inches, Estate of the artist

The Japanese attack on Pearl Harbor changed not only the course of international events; it also altered millions of individual histories. In Austin and elsewhere the effects of renewed European warfare had already been felt by December 7, 1941. The university's art department, which Ward Lockwood had built, responded to the changing international situation by introducing courses in military camouflage. A distant war had begun to intrude upon the traditional tranquility of the studio and the classroom — a tranquility which vanished with the "day of infamy."

In July, 1942, Lockwood left the University of Texas and rejoined the military, as a captain in the U. S. Army. For the remainder of the war Lockwood's military obligations kept him away from his studio and his work. In 1946 he noted that "During my war service I had no time at all for painting and now desperately feel the need for an uninterrupted stretch of work."[1] Lockwood's return to the Austin campus that year apparently did not fully satisfy his creative needs. Although doubtless pleased to be back to his teaching, the artist was concerned over "The loss of my production of paintings during the latter war years [which] has resulted in an insufficient amount of recent work to adequately participate in current exhibitions or to supply dealers. I know," he wrote, "that a year's uninterrupted work will allow me in large measure to renew my ability and replenish my production." Lockwood clearly desired to continue his artistic career, and he hoped "that the wider experience gained by circumstances that caused me to forsake painting for temporary periods may lend to it deeper human significance and greater aesthetic value."[2]

In 1947 Lockwood took a year's leave of absence from the University of Texas and began to remodel the "small house and a large studio"[3] which he had purchased outside of Taos just before the war. In addition to making a home out of what had been a bare four-room adobe house, Lockwood also worked at his painting and regained some of the confidence he had shown in the previous decade. After the war years away from the studio, his first efforts were understandably tentative. *Soldier* (fig. VI-2), painted in 1945 immediately following his discharge, is scarcely one of his more successful paintings; but it does convey, in its isolated figure and nocturnal setting, some of the same somber mood Lockwood had sought in his compositions of the immediate prewar years.

Although best remembered for his landscape motifs, Lockwood also worked with figurative paintings and even on occasion created self-portraits. A curious example of this last type is a pencil drawing (fig. VI-1) done just before the war, in which the artist gazes outward with an intense stare; the nervous tracings of the pencil seem to register personality as much as physical appearance. More obvious and heavy-handed was his 1941 canvas, *Apprehension* (fig. VI-3), with its theatrical forebodings of disaster and warfare. The dire mood suggested by this painting reappeared in a series of gruesome paintings of skeletal jugglers done in the same decade. Works like the *Red Juggler* (fig. VI-5) mark the culmination of Lockwood's efforts with this distinctive theme which he had earlier handled in less suggestive drawings (fig. VI-6). The drawing suggests affinities with the Colorado Springs mural by Andrew Dasburg (fig. VI-7), which Lockwood obviously knew and admired; but unlike the decorative charm which Dasburg brought to his mural, Lockwood's wartime jugglers evoke more forceful responses and suggest intentions less decorative than expressive or politically symbolic.

In 1948 Lockwood's New Mexico residency was interrupted again, this time by the offer of a job in the art department at the University of California, Berkeley. Back in the Bay Area, where he had taught in the summer of 1939, Lockwood continued his postwar reintroduction to teaching and studio life. Although the role of painter-teacher was generally satisfying for him, Lockwood did express occasional reservations. To Forbes Watson he reported: "I'm stealing this time to write from one of my classes — they'll probably do better on their own anyway. Often I think they should be looking over our shoulders watching us work rather than the reverse. In order to accomplish that, however, we would have to build grandstands in our studios."[4]

The tentative attitude regarding his teaching, toward which Lockwood made light-hearted comment, was also apparent in his varied paintings of the period. When the "new Lockwood" was first shown in New York, one reviewer noted: "In an overall viewing of his pictures on display, one has a feeling of lack of continuity in viewpoint."[5] While the works of the late 1940s do vary greatly in type, another critic felt that this was simply evidence that Lockwood "has never ceased to develop his native artistic equipment or to give full play to his vital imagination. Generally identified as a painter of western scenes, Lockwood's current works might suggest a decided change in motif and direction; yet, this could hardly be true, as Lockwood has never been a predictable artist. Consistently he has displayed an inventiveness that is provocative and sometimes confusing."[6]

Lockwood's indecision and a body of work at the same time provocative and confusing might be read as symptoms of the times in art and elsewhere. Reporting on a 1948 visit to New York Lockwood wrote that "it is still a wonderful and exciting place — but everything seemed over-crowded to me — 57th St. seemed over-crowded with galleries — galleries for the most part over-crowded with pictures — people's minds over-crowded with ideas. A frenetic life with little time for repose — or perhaps the whole world." Continuing with his reactions to the current situation, Lockwood described his visit to a San Francisco showing of contemporary painting. "The general state of confusion was certainly apparent in the lot of 185 things displayed [at the California Palace of the Legion of Honor]. Of course everything considered how could it be otherwise?"[7]

The artists' community in the Bay Area presented a lively scene during the postwar period. Alfred Frankenstein, long an observer of the local situation, has written that "Abstract Expressionism broke everywhere in the 1950s, but nowhere did it have greater impact than in San Francisco."[8] Supported by a sense of community and shared

91

VI-3: *Apprehension*, 1941, location unknown, photograph courtesy Archives of American Art, Smithsonian Institution

VI-4: *Disaster*, acrylic on canvas, 48 x 35½ inches, Estate of the artist

VI-5: *Red Juggler*, acrylic on masonite, 30 x 24 inches, Estate of the artist

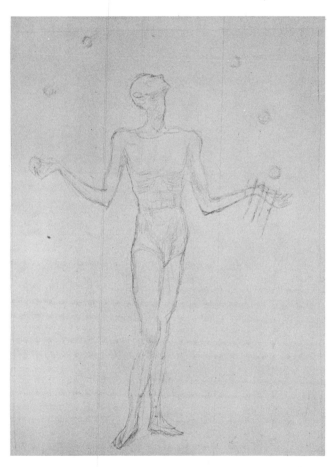

VI-6: *Juggler*, pencil, 29¼ x 21 inches, Estate of the artist

VI-7: Andrew Dasburg, *Circus Mural*, ca. 1936, detail, oil on canvas, Colorado Springs Fine Arts Center

adventure which these Bay Area artists offered — and strengthened by the time and place for contemplation which Berkeley (but not New York) offered — Lockwood ultimately regained his stride and came to enjoy a considerable reputation in the 1950s and early 1960s.

As had been the case in New Mexico, Lockwood was initially struck by the character of the California landscape. "This area is a beautiful one — and stimulating artistically too," he enthused. "We have enjoyed it on previous visits and are enjoying it again."[9] His sketchbooks contain numerous drawings of landscape and coastal motifs, some done with pen and ink in a curious linear style (fig. VI-8). This fascination with linear design and faceted shapes is found in quite another form in his *Disaster*, also done in the late 1940s (fig. VI-4). Here, in a gesture suggestive of the groping search he was conducting, Lockwood repeated a motif of several years earlier (see fig. VI-3). In the later work, however, the forceful statement implied by the 1941 canvas is largely lost in this maze of decorative faceting.

VI-8: *Coastal View*, pen and ink, Archives of American Art, Smith-sonian Institution

The drawing style of the coastal sketches was more happily translated to a series of abstractions which Lockwood produced about 1950 (see fig. VI-9). In these abstractions there is a new delicacy and a feeling for an overall, uniform image. In this the drawings show affinities with the intricate constructions etched by Ynez Johnston, whose work was admired and collected by Lockwood (fig. VI-10). The abstraction also evokes memories of Paul Klee's fantastic drawings, a source which had particular impact on Lockwood. In 1949 he wrote to a friend that he had seen, "and will see again, a retrospective show of the work of Paul Klee and in it so much sheer and poignant beauty! In such accomplishment lies the ultimate in teaching."[10]

94

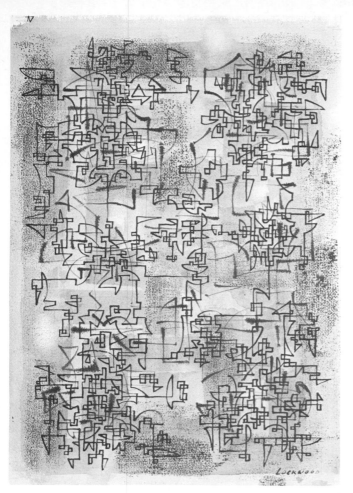

VI-9: Untitled, *ca.* 1950, tempera on paper, 29½ x 21 inches, Estate of the artist

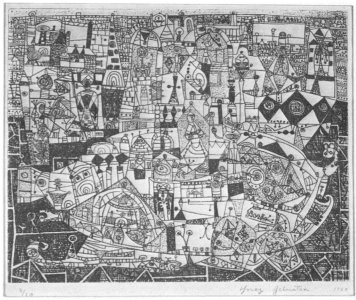

VI-10: Ynez Johnston, Untitled, 1950, etching, 8⅜ x 10⅛ inches, The University of Kansas Museum of Art, The Lockwood Collection

The delicate fantasies of Paul Klee, the expressive strength of recent abstract painting, the camaraderie of the San Francisco art community, and the challenges of the Berkeley classroom — all contributed to Lockwood's rapid development in the 1950s. The decade was marked by his turn away from the pictorial representations of the Southwest, familiar from the prewar days, to a new and abstract freedom in his handling of the medium. Equally significant was Lockwood's choice of a new medium. In the late 1940s, as he had done on earlier occasions, Lockwood showed his openness to innovation in adopting new, synthetic pigments for his work. Acrylic paint, being water-based, was more fluid and easily handled than the traditional oil medium; in this regard it was more akin to the watercolor medium in which Lockwood had done some of his finest earlier work.

In a number of his first essays with the new pigments Lockwood showed the careful control and sense of prior composition which marked his work with other media. *Monument* (fig. VI-11), done about 1950 in watercolor and mixed media, was parent to a group of similar, cellular images culminating with the *Evolving Totem*, 1954 (fig. VI-12),

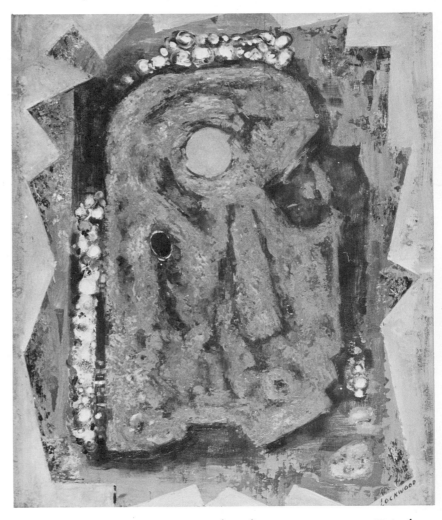

VI-11: *Monument, ca.* 1950, mixed media on paper, 23½ x 17 inches, Estate of the artist

VI-12: *Evolving Totem*, 1954, acrylic on masonite, 29¾ x 24 inches,
Estate of the artist

VI-13: *Prison Rodeo, ca,* 1948-49, acrylic on canvas, 36 x 48 inches,
Estate of the artist

VI-14: *Abstraction in Gray and Red,* 1957, acrylic on canvas, 45 x 65
inches, Estate of the artist

painted with acrylics on masonite. The balanced, centralized imagery of these works is at odds with the expansive forces and the recognizable subject matter of *Prison Rodeo, circa* 1948-49 (fig. VI-13). In this exuberant painting, which also utilizes the synthetic pigment, Lockwood has more fully realized its fluid potential. The vitality and movement of the subject are captured in the artist's colorful arrangement of schematic forms. The treatment of horses and humans is so summary and stylized as to suggest that Lockwood's interest lay with the overall sense of activity and motion, rather than with the photographic details of the scene.

Lockwood's development in the second half of the decade indicates that such was indeed the case. An untitled painting of 1957 (fig. VI-14) utilizes the same centrifugal arrangement of forms, but without any specific subject. The forces and activity, rendered explicity in *Prison Rodeo*, are here suggested but not specified.

Lockwood saw his own tendency toward abstraction, as well as that of his contemporaries, as a reflection of the external world. "I believe the present emphasis upon purely abstract art has its roots in our contemporary life and draws nourishment from a variety of human thoughts and actions throughout our world . . . Whether it be purely abstract or not," he wrote, "art has been and will be an organic, unified, and meaningful expression of what the artist feels, sees, and knows."[11] Several years later the artist reiterated this attitude, while admitting that his art "doesn't copy [the] external appearance of nature. It's an attempt to abstract from what one sees, knows and feels and to express that in individual ways."[12]

As frequently happened with converts to the abstract idiom, Lockwood's new paintings disaffected portions of his traditional audience. Lockwood noted that "In much of the contemporary art found anywhere in the world today, you will find experimentation not understood at all by the layman . . . experimentation in which artists are searching for symbols not known before."[13] Among the laymen not understanding Lockwood's innovations were the San Francisco Supervisors. When Lockwood's *Warrior with Flowers* was among the purchase prize winners at the city-subsidized San Francisco Art Festival in 1950, one Supervisor was led to declare that such selections represented "thievery of the people's money!" Other city fathers opined: "Disgraceful! Crazy stuff! If that's art, I'm a Chinese Communist. If I could get them to stop painting that way — I'd do it!" The *Chronicle* noted that "a canvass of seven Supervisors' positions show that none pretends to know about art but each knows what he likes, including primarily pictures of dogs, horses, birds, Winston Churchill and General MacArthur, and 'none of this futuristic stuff'."[14]

The Art Festival brouhaha was soon forgotten, and Lockwood shortly found a more sympathetic audience, both with the public and the press, if not with the politicians. In 1953 Alfred Frankenstein praised Lockwood not as an abstract painter, but as "a romantic who makes use of the abstractionists' discoveries for his own purposes. He is also a magnificent composer and painterly craftsman; the subtleties of his surface are fully equated with the strength of his forms, and the total effect of his work is therefore one of completely

VI-15: *Phenomenon, ca.* 1952, oil and casein on canvas, 36 x 52 inches,
Estate of the artist

ripened statement."[15] The exhibition at the San Francisco Museum of
Art, which Frankenstein reviewed, was Lockwood's first major
exposure to the Bay Area audience. Included in the exhibition were
recent paintings, such as *Phenomenon* (fig. VI-15) which showed
Lockwood's facility with the brush and palette knife to good advantage.
The sticklike forms and short strokes of paint recall the branches and
blossoms of earlier designs such as *Blossoms* (fig. VI-16), wherein the
image remains legible. In the later work it is the feeling for nature — the
suggestion of flickering leaves and filtered sunlight — which remains
as evidence of the Nature orientation at the base of Lockwood's artistry.

Later the handling of the paint grew bolder, as in *Undulations*
(PLATE X), in which the acrylic is spread with an architectural triangle;
but the feeling for space and movement and the exquisite surface
effect remain tantamount. *Undulations* was among the paintings
featured in a 1959 exhibit at the de Young Museum in San Francisco,
a show which again won the praises of the *Chronicle's* critic. He wrote
that Lockwood "does not express himself pictorially in any niggling
or miniaturistic fashion. All the Lockwoods in the show are immensely
spacious, not so much in the size of the canvases as in their implications.
They carry into the realm of the abstract that fascination with the

VI-16: *Blossoms*, oil on masonite, 16 x 20 inches, Collection of Mr. and
Mrs. Raymond Nichols

unhurried, grandly scaled world of the Southwest that has always
been characteristic of this artist . . . "[16]

Even after a decade in the San Francisco area the feeling for the
Southwest persisted in Lockwood's work. Since the Lockwoods
continued to summer at their New Mexico home it is not surprising to
find the recurrence of Taos subjects in his work; but when the abstractions bear the stamp of the limitless scale of the northern New Mexico
plateau as well, the assimilation of artist and landscape may be judged
complete. Thus, predictably one finds Lockwood seasonally migrating
to Taos, and returning there in 1962 to enjoy his retirement from
the university life.

# VII. The Return to New Mexico

**W**riting of the "leaders of the American art revolution," Ward Lockwood once observed that "practically all of them found it necessary from time to time to desert their studios for jobs in the marketplace. But these were only detours; at the first opportunity they returned to the compulsive battle between themselves and the canvases confronting them."[1]

Lockwood's own detour ended in 1962 when he returned to New Mexico to enjoy his retirement from teaching. On the occasion of an earlier sabbatical leave, he had commented that "only a painter-teacher can properly appreciate my privilege of spending long day after long day at work in my studio."[2] The Taos area to which the Lockwoods returned was scarcely the "three-bathroom town" which had greeted them in 1926. What had been a remote and small artist's colony had burgeoned into a major art and tourist center, where Lockwood counted "at least ten or a dozen galleries with work ranging all the way from aspens to abstractions — from nonimportant to nonobjective."[3]

The return to Taos marked the consummation of the artist's long affection for the remarkable New Mexican landscape. As one of his California colleagues recalled, "the real home in spirit always seemed to be Taos . . . and the landscape of Taos never ceased to be the subject matter for his paintings. In the late work this was not less true than in the early work. Lockwood was always a landscape painter, even after he became a full time studio painter."[4]

VII-1: *Memories of New Mexico*, brown conte crayon, 22 x 30 inches, Estate of the artist

VII-2: *Southwest No. 3, Katchina*, oil and casein on canvas, 36 x 52 inches, Estate of the artist

Indeed, throughout the 1950s, Lockwood's art had shown a continuing reliance upon landscape sources, especially Taos (see fig. VII-1). Even when more abstractly handled, his work of that period still refers to New Mexico; in *Red Formation* (PLATE IX), for instances, the angular shapes and the palette reflect the eroded, brick-red landscape forms of the Southwest.

The shapes and colors of that country appeared in a group of canvases which Lockwood produced in the mid-1950s. The series, called *Southwest*, was comprised of paintings with individual members and titles which were inspired by Lockwood's biannual peregrinations through the region between Berkeley and Taos. In the works the generalized forms of the landscape are often combined with stylized forms drawn from Indian motifs, to create symbols of Lockwood's world (see fig. VII-2).

The enduring attraction to New Mexico was also revealed in a series of landscape drawings which date from Lockwood's last years. These small works, done with pen or brush and ink on paper, are distillations of the landscape which convey a sense of ease and intimate familiarity with the subject. Drawn at the Lockwood home on the Talpa ridge, or at the sites in the Taos Valley, these modest works show the artist's draughtsmanship to best advantage. In some (see fig. VII-3) the line is angular and choppy, recalling the earlier coastal sketches Lockwood made in California (see fig. VI-8). In others the interest is more in the sense of scale, the terrific sweep of space of the Taos Valley, which had initially attracted Lockwood to the area. *Pine Trees and Taos Valley* (fig. VII-4) is a graphic reinterpretation of the landscape, presenting the same awesome grandeur of the country as appeared in Lockwood's early Taos efforts.

VII-3: *Canyon*, 1959, pen and ink, 15 x 21½ inches, Estate of the artist

Lockwood handled this landscape motif in varied media in his last years. The expansive sweep of the Taos Valley reappeared in *Verdant Passage*, done in acrylic (fig. VII-5), which, like the ink drawing, evokes parallels with earlier work (see PLATE VI).

*Gray Valley*, a pastel of this period, reinterprets the subject in a more subtle vein (fig. VII-6). Lockwood's friend, Loren Mozley, has written of these late works: " . . . finally, there is a series of gentle pastels, among them the last thing Ward Lockwood did. They might have served as models for later paintings which will not be painted. They seem to cross back and forth over his experiences, and to bind up, somehow, all that he had seen and done."[5] The *Gray Valley*, while depicting a familiar view, does so in an abbreviated, schematic fashion, the distilled product of long familiarity on Lockwood's behalf.

The return to New Mexico brought with it not only a renewal of traditional themes but also new explorations in unfamiliar fields.

104

VII-4: *Pine Trees and Taos Valley, ca.* 1960, pen and ink, 15⅜ x 22¼
inches, Estate of the artist

VII-5: *Verdant Passage*, 1959, acrylic on canvas, 36 x 48 inches, Estate of the artist

VII-6: *Gray Valley, ca.* 1960, pastel and crayon on paper, 14½ x 21 inches, Estate of the artist

Lockwood had worked sporadically in the graphic media, most consistently as a lithographer in the late 1920s and early 1930s. This technique gained his attention anew following his retirement, when in Talpa he produced several new prints. Like many of his works of the late period, *Crystalline* (fig. VII-7) has no specific natural reference; but in its facets and cellular imagery it suggests organic or landscape subjects which also appear, somewhat abstracted, in the paintings and pastels of the same years.

One indication of Lockwood's inventiveness was his continuing experimentation with new means and materials. In the late 1950s he briefly toyed with collage (see fig. VII-8); the decorative patterning created by the scraps of paper pleased Lockwood and several years later led to a series of collographs. From January through April, 1962, between Berkeley and Taos, Lockwood held a Visiting Professorship at the University of Washington, where he learned the collograph technique.[6] The collograph plates were made of a collage of textured surfaces, built up to low relief, which when inked and printed transferred an embossed impression to the paper. Their printed effect is not unlike the overlapping strokes of acrylic in Lockwood's paintings of the period. When the collographs like *Cruciform* (fig. VII-9) were first exhibited, critics commented that they combined concern for form, texture and abstract organization with "a great spiritual quality. His *Multiform* [fig. VII-10] is also black and gray and reminds one of torn pages, very fragmentized. There is a strong sense of the metaphysical here."[7]

The collographs and a series of junk assemblages, which also date from the early 1960s (see fig. VII-11), were the last new experiments which Lockwood was able to make. Together with the landscape drawings, the pastels, and the paintings of his later years, they show the easy coexistence of invention and tradition in Lockwood's art. In one of his last comments on his own work, Lockwood spoke of his assemblages: "To organize this miscellany — this junk — this detritus — I find a fascinating challenge." He felt that properly assembled, the pieces could "become not only aesthetically significant but [also could] express in a curious, cogent and immediate way the time and place in which we live."[8]

The opportunity for relaxed study and work which Lockwood anticipated in his retirement was ultimately denied him. Barely a year after returning to Taos, Ward Lockwood died in his Ranchos de Taos home on July 6, 1963.

Over the span of nearly fifty years, Lockwood's art had evolved in a logical, almost inevitable fashion. In the course of this career, he had grown from the "telling of stories" to the "painting of poems," from the specific views of Provence or New Mexico to the more abstract visions of his late years. Yet in the end, as at the beginning, Lockwood consistently sought to realize the essential combination of aesthetic significance and an expression of the artist's time and place. In the realization of these complementary goals lies the significance of Ward Lockwood's career.

15/17  2nd ot                    CRYSTALLINE                    LOCKWOOD

VII-7: *Crystalline, ca.* 1962, lithograph, 15¾ x 21½ inches, The University of Kansas Museum of Art, The Lockwood Collection

VII-8: Untitled, 1958, paper collage on cardboard, 26½ x 18½ inches,
Estate of the artist

VII-9: *Cruciform, ca.* 1962, collograph,
22½ x 11½ inches, Estate of the artist

VII-10: *Multiform*, 1962, collograph, 16 x 23½ inches, Estate of the artist

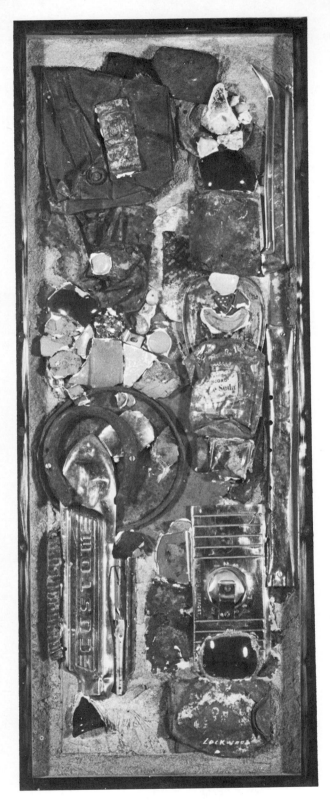

VII-11: *Custome Made, ca.* 1962-63,
    assemblage, 37⅞ x 18¾ x 1⅞ inches,
    Estate of the artist

# Color Plates

Plate I: *French Landscape, Avignon*, 1922, oil on canvas, 25¾ x 32 inches, The Whitney Museum of American Art, New York

Plate II: *Haying Time in Talpa*, 1926, oil on canvas, 25 x 30 inches, The Nelson Gallery-Atkins Museum, Kansas City, Missouri

Plate III: *Turn in the Road, Old Ledoux Street*, 1928, oil on canvas, 18 x 24 inches, The University of Kansas Museum of Art, The Lockwood Collection

Plate IV: *Street Scene, Taos, ca.* 1928-29, watercolor, 15½ x 19½ inches, The University of Kansas Museum of Art, The Lockwood Collection

Plate V: *Rio Hondo*, 1930, oil on canvas, 25 x 30 inches, The University of Kansas Museum of Art, The Lockwood Collection

Plate VI: *Magic of the Snow*, 1934, watercolor, 15½ x 20½ inches, The Dallas Museum of Fine Arts, Gift of the Lida Hooe Memorial Fund

Plate VII: *The Corner Grocery (Cisneros Store)*, 1938, oil and tempera on gessoed panel, 33 x 45 inches, The University of Kansas Museum of Art, The Lockwood Collection

Plate VIII: *Kiowa Indian Dance*, 1940, watercolor with waxed surface, 21 x 31½ inches, The University of Kansas Museum of Art, The Lockwood Collection

Plate IX: *Red Formation, ca. 1956*, oil and casein on canvas, 30 x 40 inches, Estate of the artist

Plate X: *Undulations, ca.* 1958-59, acrylic on canvas, 50 x 69 inches, Estate of the artist

# NOTES AND BIBLIOGRAPHY

# NOTES

## I. "An Artist's Roots"

1. Ward Lockwood, in *Ward Lockwood: A Retrospective Exhibition of Paintings, Prints and Drawings* (Austin: University Art Museum, University of Texas, 1967), p. 4.

2. Ward Lockwood, "An Artist's Roots," *Magazine of Art*, 33:5 (May, 1940), p. 268.

3. *Ibid.*, p. 269.

4. See Milton W. Brown, *American Painting from the Armory Show to the Depression* (Princeton, 1970), pp. 71-76, for a discussion of "The War Years."

5. Lockwood, "An Artist's Roots," p. 269.

6. Brown, p. 76.

7. Lockwood, "An Artist's Roots," p. 269.

8. *Ibid.*

9. *Ibid.*

10. Quoted in "Wonderful World of Atchison Boy," June 25, 1922, unidentified newspaper clipping; Lockwood Papers, Archives of American Art, roll 534, frame 678. Hereafter, AAA, roll/frame.

11. Lockwood, "Art Student's Life in Paris," *The Atchison Daily Globe*, May 31, 1921; AAA, 534/673.

12. Lockwood, "An Artist's Roots," p. 269.

13. Lockwood, "Foreword" to catalogue for *Exhibition of Paintings by J. Ward Lockwood* (Topeka, Kansas: Washburn College, 1922), n.p.

14. Lockwood, "An Artist's Roots," p. 269.

15. Lockwood, "Intuition and the Art Spirit" (manuscript for a lecture), n.d.; AAA, 534/424-425.

16. That his reputation was more than local was suggested by at least one French publication, which proclaimed that "J. Ward Lockwood can be classed head and shoulder above others, as an outstanding figure in the category of modern American painters." ("J. Ward Lockwood," *Revue du vrai et du beau* (Paris), undated clipping (ca. 1925?); AAA, 534/1079.

17. Lockwood, "An Artist's Roots," p. 272.

## II. Taos: Creative Freedom

1. Quoted in Thomas Thompson, "Turnstile," *Amarillo Globe-Times (Texas)*, August 30, 1961, p. 2.

2. Blumenschein, unpublished manuscript, quoted in James Gaither, "A Return to the Village: A Study of Santa Fe and Taos, New Mexico, as Cultural Centers, 1900-1934," unpublished Ph.D. thesis, University of Minnesota, Minneapolis, 1957, p. 107.

3. Quoted in Dorothy Skousen Black, "A Study of Taos as an Art Colony and of Representative Taos Painters," unpublished M.A. thesis, University of New Mexico, Albuquerque, 1959, p. 8.

4. Charlotte Leon Mayerson, ed., *Shadow and Light: The Life, Friends and Opinions of Maurice Sterne* (New York, 1965), p. 137.

5. Frieda Lawrence, *Memoirs and Correspondence*, ed. by E. W. Tedlock (London, 1961), p. 112.

6. Cowley, "An Afterword on the Modern Mind," in *Books That Have Mattered*, ed. by Malcolm Cowley and Bernard Smith (New York, 1939), p. 240.

7. "Paintings of the West," *El Palacio*, 8:7-8 (July, 1920), p. 235.

8. Kenneth M. Adams, "Los Ocho Pintores," *New Mexico Quarterly*, XXI:2 (Summer, 1951), p. 148.

9. Ward Lockwood, "Taos Arts: Exciting Country, Extraordinary People Attracted Ward Lockwood," *The Taos (N.M.) News*, May 31, 1962, p. 5.

10. *Ibid.*

11. M.K.P., "Art" (review of Lockwood exhibition at the Conrad Hug Galleries, Kansas City, Mo.) *Kansas City Star*, March 26, 1929; AAA, 534/689.

12. Maynard Walker, "New Hug Exhibit is Refreshing" (review of Lockwood exhibition at the Conrad Hug Galleries, Kansas City, Mo.), Feb. 27, 1927; AAA, 534/681.

13. "An Original Conception of the Taos Community" (review of Lockwood exhibition at the Conrad Hug Galleries, Kansas City, Mo.), *Kansas City Journal Post*, Feb. 20, 1927; AAA, 534/683.

14. Walker, "New Hug Exhibit is Refreshing"; AAA, 534/680.

15. Quoted in Polly Noyes, "Taos — 100 Miles of Fascination," *San Francisco Chronicle*, Aug. 13, 1950, p. 4-L.

16. Andrew Dasburg, "Notes," in *Andrew Dasburg* (Dallas Museum of Fine Arts, 1957), [p. 13].

17. Mabel Dodge Luhan, *Taos and Its Artists* (New York, 1947), p. 16.

18. Statement by Ward Lockwood, in *Andrew Dasburg*, [p. 23].

19. The early date of this painting is suggested by the signature — "J. Ward Lockwood" — which, like the French but unlike most of the New Mexican works, uses the first initial. Furthermore, the style of the painting is characterized by the broad handling of pigment and strong lights of *Haying Time in Talpa*, also done in 1926.

20. Dasburg, "Notes," in *Andrew Dasburg*, [p. 15].

21. Mabel Dodge Luhan, "Taos — A Eulogy," *Creative Art*, 9 (October, 1931), p. 293.

22. Luhan, *Taos and Its Artists*, p. 16.

23. Statement by Ward Lockwood, in *Andrew Dasburg*, [p. 21].

24. Ward Lockwood, "Report from New Mexico," *San Francisco Art Association Bulletin*, 18:4-5 (April-May, 1952), n.p.

25. Ruth Green Harris, "A Round of Galleries," *New York Times*, January 12, 1930, p. 12-X.

26. John Marin, *Selected Writings of John Marin*, ed. by Dorothy Norman (New York, 1949), p. 127.

27. MacKinley Helm, *John Marin* (New York. 1948), p. 64.

28. Lockwood, "The Marin I Knew: A Personal Reminiscence," *Texas Quarterly*, X:1 (Spring, 1967), p. 107.

29. Luhan, *Taos and Its Artists*, p. 38.

30. Interview with Gina Knee (Mrs. Alexander Brook), June 17, 1973.

31. Statement by Loren Mozley, in *Andrew Dasburg*, [p. 24].

32. Lockwood, "The Marin I Knew," p. 107.

33. Lockwood, "Fellow Artist and Longtime Friend Reviews Higgins' Fine Exhibition," *El Crepusculo*, August 30, 1956; AAA, 534/876.

34. Marin, *Selected Writings of John Marin*, p. 129.

35. Letter to the author, March 13, 1973.

36. "Ward Lockwood Explains Trend in Modern Art" (unidentified newspaper clipping, *circa* May 1932); AAA, 534/1016.

37. Interview with the artist, June 23, 1970.

38. Lockwood Journal, August 4, 1931; AAA, 534/348. Lockwood's writing style in this entry is curiously reminiscent of John Marin's unique syntax.

39. "Exhibitions in New York: Ward Lockwood," *Art News*, XXXIX:32 (May 9, 1931), p. 12.

40. "Attractions in Other Galleries," *New York Sun*, May 9, 1931; AAA, 534/699.

41. Review of Lockwood exhibition, May 10, 1931; AAA, 534/699.

42. Ward Lockwood to his parents (?), n.d.; AAA, 534/338.


## III. Taos: A Landscape's Power

1. Ralph Flint, "Post-Impressionism," in *America and Alfred Stieglitz*, ed. Waldo Frank *et al.* (New York, 1934), pp. 169-170.

2. Matthew Baigell, *A History of American Painting* (New York, 1971), p. 215.

3. Van Deren Coke, *Taos and Santa Fe: The Artist's Environment 1882-1942* (Albuquerque, 1963), p. 110.

4. Luhan, *Taos and Its Artists*, p. 38.

5. Kyle Crichton, "Cease Not Living," *The New Mexico Quarterly*, V (May, 1935), p. 76.

6. Mabel Luhan, *Winter in Taos* (Denver, 1935), pp. 85-86.

7. Lockwood Journal, February 24, 1933; AAA, 534/360.

8. Ward Lockwood, "Taos Arts: Exciting Country, Extraordinary People Attracted Ward Lockwood," *The Taos (N.M.) News*, May 24, 1962, p. 13.

9. James Gray, "Ward Lockwood's Art," *St. Paul (Minnesota) Dispatch*, December 15, 1932: AAA, 534/719.

10. Interview with Gina Knee, June 17, 1973.

11. Lockwood, "Taos Arts: Exciting Country . . . ," (May 24, 1962), p. 13.

12. Quoted in Ralph Purcell, *Government and Art: A Study of American Experience* (Washington, D.C., 1956), pp. 70-71. Whatever its aesthetic merits might have been, American Scene painting clearly made good politics.

13. Patricia Trenton, *Picturesque Images from Taos and Santa Fe* (Denver Art Museum, 1974), p. 143.

14. Duncan Pollock, "Artists of Taos and Santa Fe: from Zane Grey to the Tide of Modernism," *Art News*, 73:1 (January, 1974), p. 21.

15. Lockwood to Edward B. Rowan, Superintendent, Treasury Department Section of Painting and Sculpture, October 20, 1937. Washington, D.C., Post Office Department Building, Public Buildings Administration Records, National Archives Building, Washington, D.C. (hereafter cited as PBA/NA). Also, AAA, 534/165.

16. Lockwood to Olin Dows, November 1, 1937; Watson Papers, AAA, D-56/350.

17. Lockwood to Forbes Watson, August 31, 1938; Watson Papers, AAA, D-56/335.

## IV. For the People: Lockwood Murals

1. Lockwood Journal; AAA, 534/358.

2. Francis V. O'Connor, *Federal Support for the Visual Arts: The New Deal and Now*, (Greenwich, Conn., 1969), p. 16.

3. Biddle, quoted in O'Connor, pp. 17-18.

4. Richard D. McKinzie, *The New Deal for Artists* (Princeton, 1973), p. 6.

5. Rowan, quoted in McKinzie, p. 23.

6. Bruce, quoted in McKinzie, p. 57.

7. Rowan, quoted in McKinzie, p. 23.

8. Bruce, quoted in McKinzie, p. 57.

9. *Ibid.*

10. W.P.A. Writers' Program, *New Mexico: A Guide to the Colorful State*, (New York, 1946), p. 222.

11. Lockwood to Edward B. Rowan, April 5, 1936; Washington, D.C.: Post Office Department Building, PBA/NA. Also, AAA, 534/87-88.

12. Lewis W. Rubenstein, "Fresco Painting Today," *The American Scholar*, 4:4 (Autumn, 1935), pp. 419, 427.

13. Rubenstein, p. 419.

14. Lockwood to Edward B. Rowan, October 7, 1935; Wichita, Kansas: Post Office, PBA/NA.

15. Lockwood, "Account of the Post Office frescoes"; Washington, D.C.: Post Office Department Building, PBA/NA.

16. See Lockwood letters to Edward B. Rowan, December 16, 1935, and January 18, 1937. Washington, D.C.: Post Office Department Building, PBA/NA. (The letter of December 16, 1935, is also in AAA, 534/70-71.)

17. Lockwood to Edward B. Rowan, March 27, 1937; Washington, D.C.: Post Office Department Building, PBA/NA. Also, AAA, 534/136-137.

18. Rowan to Lockwood, April 7, 1937; Washington, D.C.: Post Office Department Building, PBA/NA.

19. Memorandum of Olin Dows trip to New York, May 1, 1936, quoted in McKinzie, p.60.

20. Handwritten note by Mr. LaFarge on memorandum from Edward B. Rowan to Section staff, October 13, 1936; Washington, D.C.: Post Office Department Building, PBA/NA.

21. Lockwood to Edward B. Rowan, March 27, 1937; Washington, D.C.: Post Office Department Building, PBA/NA.

22. *Ibid.*

23. See Alfred Haworth Jones, "The Search for a Usable American Past in the New Deal Era," *American Quarterly*, 25:3 (December, 1971), pp. 710-724.

24. John Dos Passos, *The Ground We Stand On: Some Examples from the History of a Political Creed* (New York, 1941), p. 3.

25. Jones, p. 715.

26. Lockwood to Edward B. Rowan, March 27, 1937; Washington, D.C.: Post Office Department Building, PBA/NA.

27. *Ibid.*

28. *Ibid.*

29. *Ibid.*

30. *Ibid.*

31. Lockwood Journal, October 30, 1931; AAA, 534/353.

32. E. A. Jewell, "In the Realm of Art: Capitol Walls and Other Matters," *New York Times*, December 21, 1941, p. X-9.

33. Dufy, cited in a script for a slide lecture; Forbes Watson Papers, AAA, D-56/361.

34. *Ibid.*

35. Rowan to Lockwood, September 16, 1937; Washington, D.C.: Post Office Department Building, PBA/NA.

36. C. A. Seward to Edward B. Rowan, May 14, 1935; Wichita, Kansas: Post Office, PBA/NA.

37. C. A. Seward to Lockwood, August 2, 1935; Wichita, Kansas: Post Office, PBA/NA.

38. Lockwood to Edward B. Rowan, August 20, 1935; Wichita, Kansas: Post Office, PBA/NA.

39. "American Theater Depicted in Panels by Ward Lockwood in Fine Arts Center Lounge," *Colorado Springs Gazette*, December 3, 1936, p. 5.

40. *Ibid.*

41. Lockwood to Edward Rowan, November 10, 1937; Lexington, Kentucky: Post Office, PBA/NA. Also, AAA, 534/171-172.

42. Lockwood to Rowan, December 9, 1937; Lexington, Kentucky: Post Office, PBA/NA. Also, AAA, 534/180-181.

43. Jones, p. 718.

44. John F. Day, "Daniel Boone Looks on Kentucky — and on Federal Justice," *The Lexington Leader*, June 8, 1938, p. 1.

45. Rowan to Lockwood, March 22, 1938; Lexington, Kentucky: Post Office, PBA/NA.

46. Rowan to Lockwood, January 21, 1938; Lexington, Kentucky: Post Office, PBA/NA. Also, AAA, 534/196.

47. Lockwood to Edward B. Rowan, January 25, 1938; Lexington, Kentucky: Post Office, PBA/NA.

48. Lockwood to Edward Rowan, December 9, 1937; *op. cit.*

49. Rowan to Edward Bruce, June 15, 1938; Lexington, Kentucky: Post Office, PBA/NA.

50. Rowan to Lockwood, September 15, 1942; Lexington, Kentucky: Post Office, PBA/NA.

51. Rowan to Edward Bruce, June 15, 1938; *op. cit.*

52. Lockwood to Edward B. Rowan, August 30, 1941; Hamilton, Texas: Post Office, PBA/NA.

53. "Texas Ranger Camp Brings Color and Atmosphere to Post Office," *The Hamilton Herald Record* (Texas), May 29, 1942, p. 1.

## V. Austin: A University Experiment

1. Ward Lockwood, "Taos Arts: Exciting Country . . . ," (May 31, 1962), p. 3.

2. *Ibid.*

3. Frank Waters, quoted in Van Deren Coke, *Taos and Santa Fe*, p. 103.

4. Ward Lockwood, "Andrew Dasburg: An Appreciation," *El Palacio*, 66:6 (December, 1959), p. 199.

5. Lockwood to Forbes Watson, October 20, 1937; Audiovisual Archives Division, National Archives, Record Group 121, Box 10.

6. For *Siesta*, Lockwood recorded the use of varied media: "July 11, 1940 Painting, Siesta on Johns Manville 'Flexboard' panel covered with 1 coat gelatin glue *[indeciperable]* coats gesso sealed with spray of 4% formalin solution — drawn in with charcoal — then drawn with diluted India ink — imprimatura of ivory black and bit of terre verde *lightly* washed over drawing with glazing medium made very thin with turpentine (so it was dull and did not shine). Then first under painting made with egg tempera (no oil) and zinc white, ivory black and terre verte used in this coat. — The next day a light gelatin glue solution thinly brushed over the whole and then sprayed with a 4% formalin solution gone over with ochre and white then gelatined and formalined again. — Color applied with glazing medium and oil paint — heightened with zinc white — oil — white with egg and water — and white with casein (sets very quickly) — varnished with Vibert retouching varnish." AAA, 534/571.

7. Ward Lockwood, "A New Way to Paint with Watercolor," manuscript, 1941; AAA, 534/395.

8. *Ibid*; AAA, 534/405.

9. *Ibid*; AAA, 534/406.

10. Lockwood, "Taos Arts: Exciting Country . . . ," (May 31, 1962), p. 3.

## VI. Berkeley: Process and Instruction

1. Lockwood to Forbes Watson, October 29, 1946; Watson Papers, AAA, D-56/353.

2. Lockwood, draft of a grant application to an unknown source, *ca.* 1946; AAA, 534/8.

3. Lockwood, "Report from New Mexico," n.p.

4. Lockwood to Forbes Watson, December 12, 1948; Watson Papers, AAA, D-56/358.

5. C. W., "Exhibitions — Solo and Group," *The New York Sun*, March 25, 1949; AAA, 534/807.

6. Marynell Sharp, "Controlled Vitality," *Art Digest*, April 1, 1949, p. 16.

7. Lockwood to Forbes Watson, December 6, 1948; Watson Papers, AAA, D-56/356-357.

8. Alfred Frankenstein, "1950-1970", in *A Century of California Painting, 1870-1970* (Los Angeles: Crocker-Citizens National Bank, 1970), p. 20.

9. Lockwood to Forbes Watson, December 6, 1948; Watson Papers, AAA, D-56/357.

10. Lockwood to Everett Spruce, April 5, 1949; AAA, 534/283.

11. Lockwood to Carl Francassini, May 1, 1951; AAA, 534/300.

12. Gordon Martin, "He's Back Where he Started in 1912," *Topeka State Journal*, November 5, 1957; AAA, 534/911.

13. Bob Sanford, "Mystery in His Exhibits at K.U. Art Museum" unidentified newspaper clipping, *ca.* 1957; AAA, 534/908.

14. "Supervisors, Modern Art Mix It Up," *The San Francisco Chronicle*, December 7, 1950; AAA, 534-833.

15. Alfred Frankenstein, "The Drawings of Charles Stafford Duncan — And Other Art Exhibits," *The San Francisco Chronicle*, January 18, 1953, p. 30.

16. Alfred Frankenstein, "Five Artists Provide a Lively Show at the deYoung," *The San Francisco Sunday Chronicle*, March 8, 1959, p. 25.

## VII: The Return to New Mexico

1. Lockwood, "Andrew Dasburg: An Appreciation," *El Palacio*, 66:6 (December, 1959), p. 200.

2. Lockwood, "Report from New Mexico," n.p.

3. *Ibid.*

4. John Haley, "California Years," in *Ward Lockwood: A Retrospective Exhibition . . .* , p. 14.

5. Loren Mozley, "In Retrospect, Ward Lockwood," in *Ward Lockwood: A Retrospective Exhibition . . .* , p. 12.

6. Lockwood statement; AAA, 534/443.

7. Helen Peterson, "About the Arts," *The New Mexican* (Santa Fe), December 2, 1963, p. 3.

8. Lockwood statement; AAA, 534/442.

# BIBLIOGRAPHY

*Publications by Ward Lockwood*

"Art Student's Life in Paris," *The Atchison Daily Globe* (Kansas), May 31, 1921.

"Foreword," *Exhibition of Paintings by J. Ward Lockwood*, Topeka, Kansas: Washburn College, 1922.

"An Artist's Roots," *The Arts*, 33:5 (May 1940), 268-273.

"Report from New Mexico," *San Francisco Art Association Bulletin*, 18:4-5 (April-May 1952).

Statement in catalogue of Andrew Dasburg exhibition, Dallas Museum of Fine Arts, 1957.

"Andrew Dasburg: An Appreciation," *El Palacio*, 66:6 (December 1959), 199-200.

"Taos Arts: Exciting Country, Extraordinary People Attracted Ward Lockwood," *The Taos News* (New Mexico), May 24, 1962, 12-13, and May 31, 1962, 3.

"The Marin I Knew: A Personal Reminiscence," *Texas Quarterly*, X:1 (Spring 1967), 107-112.

Statements in catalogue of Ward Lockwood exhibition, Austin, University Art Museum, University of Texas, 1967.


*Unpublished Writings by Ward Lockwood*

Archives of American Art, Smithsonian Institution, Washington, D.C.: Ward Lockwood's Journal, 1931-1933; "Intuition and the Art Spirit" (lecture manuscript); "A New Way of Painting with Watercolor," 1941 (manuscript); miscellaneous correspondence, 1913-1961, and undated.

National Archives (Audiovisual Archives Division), Washington, D.C.: correspondence regarding mural commissions (Record Group 121).

National Archives (Civil Archives Division), Washington, D.C.: correspondence regarding mural commissions, in records of the Public Buildings Administration.

University Archives, University of Kansas, Lawrence: miscellaneous correspondence, clippings, etc.

# COLLECTIONS

Lockwood's work is represented in many public and private collections in this country, including:

Addison Gallery of American Art, Andover, Massachusetts
Baker University, Baldwin, Kansas
Baltimore Museum of Art
California Palace of the Legion of Honor, San Francisco
Dallas Museum of Fine Arts
Delaware Art Museum, Wilmington
Denver Art Museum
Harwood Foundation, Taos, New Mexico
Henry Gallery, University of Washington, Seattle
Kansas State University, Manhattan
Marion Koogler McNay Museum of Art, San Antonio, Texas
Metropolitan Museum of Art, New York
Museum of Fine Arts, Boston
Nelson Gallery — Atkins Museum, Kansas City, Missouri
Pennsylvania Academy of the Fine Arts, Philadelphia
The Phillips Collection, Washington, D.C.
San Francisco Museum of Art
Santa Barbara Museum of Art, Santa Barbara, California
University Art Museum, University of California, Berkeley
University Art Museum, University of New Mexico, Albuquerque
University Art Museum, University of Texas, Austin
University of Kansas Museum of Art, Lawrence
Whitney Museum of American Art, New York

# ONE MAN SHOWS

Washburn College, Topeka, Kansas, 1922
Atchison Girls Club, Atchison, Kansas, 1922
Findlay Art Galleries, Kansas City, Missouri, 1922
Conrad Hug Gallery, Kansas City, Missouri, 1927 and 1929
Whitney Studio Gallery, New York, 1929

135

Topeka Art Guild Galleries, Topeka, Kansas, 1930
Denver Art Museum, 1930
Frank K. M. Rehn Galleries, New York, 1931
Mulvane Art Museum, Washburn College, Topeka, Kansas, 1931
Broadmoor Art Academy, Colorado Springs, Colorado, 1932
St. Paul School of Art, St. Paul, Minnesota, 1932
Highland Park Gallery, Dallas, 1935
Museum of Fine Arts, Houston, 1935
Witte Memorial Museum, San Antonio, 1935
Quest Art Gallery, Chicago, 1935
Gimbel Gallery of Contemporary Art, Philadelphia, 1936
Mulvane Art Gallery, Washburn College, Topeka, Kansas, 1936
Junior League Gallery, Tulsa, 1936
Santa Fe Museum, Santa Fe, 1936
City Art Museum, San Francisco, 1938
University of Texas, Austin, 1938
Museum of Fine Arts, Houston, 1941
Joseph Luyber Galleries, New York, 1949
The Art Gallery, Santa Fe, 1949
La Galeria Escondida, Taos, New Mexico, 1949 and 1951
Jonson Art Gallery, University of New Mexico, Albuquerque, 1952
San Francisco Museum of Art, San Francisco, 1953
Western Association of Art Museum Directors Traveling Exhibition, 1953
University of Texas, Austin, 1953
Mulvane Art Museum, Washburn University, Topeka, Kansas, 1954
E. B. Crocker Art Gallery, Sacramento, California, 1954
La Galeria Escondida, Taos, New Mexico, 1954
Junior League Gallery, Houston, 1957
University of Kansas Museum of Art, Lawrence, 1957
Sandzen Memorial Art Gallery, Lindsborg, Kansas, 1958
Nelson Gallery — Atkins Museum, Kansas City, Missouri, 1958
Wichita Art Association, Wichita, Kansas, 1958
M. H. de Young Memorial Museum, San Francisco, 1959
Pasadena Art Museum, Pasadena, California, 1960
Museum of New Mexico, Santa Fe, 1960
Kroeber Hall, University of California, Berkeley, 1960
Realities Gallery, Taos, New Mexico, 1960
La Galeria Escondida, Taos, New Mexico, 1961 and 1962
Artist's Gallery, Ranchos de Taos, New Mexico, 1963
University Art Museum, University of Texas, Austin, 1967 (subsequently at The Amon Carter Museum of Western Art, Fort Worth; University of California, Berkeley; University of Kansas Museum of Art, Lawrence; The University Art Museum, University of New Mexico, Albuquerque; Colorado Springs Fine Arts Center, Colorado Springs, Colorado)
The Stables Gallery of the Taos Art Association, Taos, New Mexico, 1970

*1921*

American Art Association Exhibition, Paris
Salon d'Automne, Paris

*1924*

Kansas City Art Institute, Kansas City, Missouri, Midwestern
    Artists Exhibition

*1925*

Anderson Galleries, New York, Society of the Salons of America
    Spring Exhibition
Independent Society of Artists Exhibition, New York

*1928*

California Palace of the Legion of Honor, San Francisco, Southwest
    Exhibition
Corcoran Gallery of Art, Washington, D.C., 11th Exhibition of
    Contemporary American Oil Paintings

*1929*

Carnegie Institute, Pittsburgh, Annual International Exhibition
    of Paintings
Pennsylvania Academy of the Fine Arts, Philadelphia, 124th Annual
    Exhibition

*1930*

Art Institute of Chicago, 2nd International Exhibition of Lithography
    and Wood Engraving
Carnegie Institute, Pittsburgh, Annual International Exhibition
    of Paintings
Denver Art Museum, 36th Annual Exhibition of Colorado Artists
Newark Museum, Modern American Watercolors

*1931*

Art Institute of Chicago, 11th International Exhibition: Watercolors,
    Pastels, Drawings, Monotypes and Miniatures
Brooklyn Museum, Exhibition of the American Federation of Arts
Carnegie Institute, Pittsburgh, Annual International Exhibition
    of Paintings

Colorado Springs Fine Arts Center, Artists West of the Mississippi
E. Weyhe Gallery, New York, Print Show: The United States in
    Pictures
Fair Park Gallery, Dallas, 46th Annual Exhibition of Paintings, Sculp-
    ture and Art Objects
Faulkner Memorial Art Gallery, Santa Barbara, California, Paintings by
    Taos and Santa Fe Artists
St. Paul School of Art, St. Paul, Minnesota, Modern Paintings in Twin
    Cities Collections

*1932*

Art Institute of Chicago, 12th Annual International Exhibition: Water-
    colors, Pastels, Drawings and Monotypes
Art Institute of Chicago, 45th Annual Exhibition of American Paintings
    and Sculpture
California Palace of the Legion of Honor, San Francisco, 1st Annual
    Exhibition of Western Watercolor Painting
Corcoran Gallery of Art, Washington, D.C., 13th Exhibition of
    Contemporary American Oil Paintings
Denver Art Museum, 38th Annual Exhibition of Colorado Artists
The Art Alliance, Philadelphia, Latest Work of American Print Makers
Whitney Museum of American Art, New York, 1st Biennial Exhibition
    of Contemporary American Painting

*1933*

Whitney Museum of American Art, New York, 1st Biennial Exhibition
    of Contemporary American Sculpture, Watercolors and Prints

*1934*

Pennsylvania Academy of the Fine Arts, Philadelphia, 129th Annual
    Exhibition
Whitney Museum of American Art, New York, 2nd Biennial Exhibition
    of Contemporary American Painting

*1935*

Art Institute of Chicago, 5th International Exhibition of Lithography
    and Wood Engraving
Art Institute of Chicago, 46th Annual Exhibition of American Paintings
    and Sculpture
Colorado Springs Fine Arts Center, Artists West of the Mississippi
Corcoran Gallery of Art, Washington, D.C., Biennial Exhibition of
    Contemporary Oil Paintings

*1936*

Art Institute of Chicago, 15th International Exhibition: Watercolors,
    Pastels, Drawings and Monotypes
Colorado Springs Fine Arts Center, Artists West of the Mississippi
Kansas City Art Institute, Kansas City, Missouri, Midwestern Artists
    Exhibition

Whitney Museum of American Art, New York, Treasury Department
Art Projects: Sculpture and Paintings for Federal Buildings
Whitney Museum of American Art, New York, 2nd Biennial Exhibition
of Watercolors and Pastels
Whitney Museum of American Art, New York, 3rd Biennial Exhibition
of Contemporary American Painting

*1937*

Art Institute of Chicago, 48th Annual Exhibition of American Paintings
and Sculpture
Dallas Museum of Fine Arts, Art of the Americas: Pre-Columbian and
Contemporary
Los Angeles County Fair Gallery, Pomona, California, The Theodore
B. Modra Memorial Exhibition of Art
Venice Biennale

*1938*

Pennsylvania Academy of the Fine Arts, Philadelphia, 133rd Annual
Exhibition

*1939*

Corcoran Gallery of Art, Washington, D.C., 16th Biennial Exhibition
of Contemporary American Oil Paintings
Pennsylvania Academy of the Fine Arts, Philadelphia, 134th Annual
Exhibition
Whitney Museum of American Art, New York, Contemporary Ameri-
can Watercolors

*1940*

Cranbrook Academy, Bloomfield Hills, Michigan, Cranbrook-Life
Exhibition of Contemporary American Paintings
Dallas Museum of Fine Arts, Texas General Exhibition
Washington, D.C., Art Week Exhibition
Whitney Museum of American Art, New York, Mural Designs for
Federal Buildings

*1941*

Dallas Museum of Fine Arts, 1st Annual Texas Print Exhibition

*1942*

Metropolitan Museum of Art, New York, Artists for Victory Exhibition

*1943*

Dallas Museum of Fine Arts, Texas General Exhibition

*1946*

Dallas Museum of Fine Arts, Texas General Exhibition
Whitney Museum of American Art, New York, Biennial Exhibition of
Watercolors and Sculpture

*1947*

Colorado Springs Fine Arts Center, Artists West of the Mississippi

*1948*

Colorado Springs Fine Arts Center, Artists West of the Mississippi

*1949*

Brooklyn Museum, International Watercolor Exhibition
M. H. de Young Memorial Museum, San Francisco
Nebraska Art Association, Lincoln, Annual Exhibition
San Francisco Museum of Art, San Francisco Art Association Annual
    Exhibition
Walnut Creek, California, Annual Exhibition

*1950*

Addison Gallery, Andover, Massachusetts
California Palace of the Legion of Honor, San Francisco, San Francisco
    Art Festival
Colorado Springs Fine Arts Center, Artists West of the Mississippi
Dayton Art Institute, Dayton, Ohio, Invitational Exhibition
Kansas State College, Manhattan, Regional Exhibition of Friends of Art
M. H. de Young Memorial Museum, San Francisco, Open Exhibition of
    San Francisco Art Association
Metropolitan Museum of Art, New York, American Painting Today
Museum of New Mexico, Santa Fe, 4th New Mexico Exhibition of
    Prints and Drawings
Museum of New Mexico, Santa Fe, 37th Annual Exhibition of Painters
    and Sculptors of New Mexico
Pittsburg, Kansas, Exhibition of Kansas Painters
Walker Art Center, Minneapolis, Annual Exhibition
Walnut Creek, California, Annual Exhibition
Whitney Museum of American Art, New York, Biennial Exhibition of
    Contemporary American Sculpture, Watercolors and Drawings

*1951*

La Galeria Escondida, Taos, New Mexico, Dasburg/Lockwood/Ribak
Museum of New Mexico, Santa Fe, 5th Exhibition of Graphic Arts
    in New Mexico
Museum of New Mexico, Santa Fe, 38th Annual Exhibition for New
    Mexico Artists
San Francisco Museum of Art, San Francisco, New Works by Area
    Artists
San Francisco Museum of Art, San Francisco, 15th Annual Drawing
    and Print Exhibition

University of Illinois, Urbana, Contemporary American Painting and
    Sculpture
Walnut Creek, California, Annual Exhibition

1952

Colorado Springs Fine Arts Center, Taos Painting: Yesterday and
    Today
Denver Art Museum, Man at Work
Denver Art Museum, 58th Annual Exhibition of Western Art
Metropolitan Museum of Art, New York, American Watercolors,
    Drawings and Prints
Museum of New Mexico, Santa Fe, 39th Annual Exhibition for New
    Mexico Artists
San Francisco Museum of Art, 16th Annual Drawing and Prints
    Exhibition of the San Francisco Art Association
San Francisco Museum of Art, 71st Annual Painting and Sculpture
    Exhibition of the San Francisco Art Association
University of Illinois, Urbana, Contemporary American Painting and
    Sculpture
Whitney Museum of American Art, New York, Biennial Exhibition of
    Contemporary American Sculpture, Watercolors and Drawings

1954

Dallas Museum of Fine Arts, State Fair Art Exhibition
Museum of New Mexico, Santa Fe, Annual Exhibition for New
    Mexico Artists
San Francisco Museum of Art, 73rd Annual Painting and Sculpture
    Exhibition of the San Francisco Art Association
Santa Rosa Festival of Fine Art, Santa Rosa, California
University of Illinois, Urbana, Contemporary American Painting and
    Sculpture
Whitney Museum of American Art, New York, Annual Exhibition of
    Contemporary American Sculpture, Watercolors and Drawings

1955

University of Illinois, Urbana, Contemporary American Painting and
    Sculpture
University of Utah, Salt Lake City, Western Invitational Exhibition

1956

Museum of New Mexico, Santa Fe, Annual Exhibition for New Mexico
    Artists
Museum of New Mexico, Santa Fe, Taos Moderns
San Francisco Museum of Art, 75th Annual Painting and Sculpture
    Exhibition of the San Francisco Art Association

*1957*

Art Institute of Chicago, 17th Annual Exhibition for the Society of
    Contemporary Art
Chico State College, Chico, California, University of California
    Faculty Exhibition
Museum of New Mexico, Santa Fe, Taos Moderns
New Mexico Highlands University, Las Vegas, 1st Annual Invitation
    Exhibition of New Mexico Artists
San Jose State College, San Jose, California, Centennial Art Exhibition:
    California Artists 1957
San Francisco Museum of Art, Painting and Sculpture Now
San Francisco Museum of Art, 76th Annual Painting and Sculpture
    Exhibition of the San Francisco Art Association
University of Utah, Provo, 3rd Annual Invitational Exhibition

*1958*

Amarillo, Texas, Fairgrounds, Tri-State Invitational Art Exhibition
Kansas State College, Manhattan, 5th Friends of Art Biennial Exhibition
M. H. de Young Memorial Museum, San Francisco, Fresh Paint
    Exhibition
New Mexico Highlands University, Las Vegas, 2nd Annual Invitational
    Exhibition of New Mexico Artists
Provincetown Arts Festival, Provincetown, Massachusetts
San Francisco Museum of Art, 22nd Annual Drawing and Print
    Exhibition of the San Francisco Art Association

*1959*

Colorado Springs Fine Arts Center, Artists West of the Mississippi
Colorado Springs Fine Arts Center, Contemporary Art Society
    Exhibition
Museum of New Mexico, Santa Fe, Taos Moderns
Stables Gallery, Taos, New Mexico, Travelling Exhibition of Taos
    Painters
University of Illinois, Urbana, Contemporary American Painting
    and Sculpture

*1960*

Amarillo, Texas, Fairgrounds, Tri-State Invitational Art Exhibition
California Palace of the Legion of Honor, San Francisco, Winter
    Invitational Exhibition
Museum of New Mexico, Santa Fe, Taos Moderns

*1962*

Barn Annex, Taos, New Mexico, Group Exhibition of Taos Artists

*1963*

Denver Art Museum
Fort Worth Museum, Travelling Exhibition of Taos Painters